Furniture Finishing

By the Editors of Sunset and Southern Living

Paste wood filler *is mixed with black and red japan colors. Custom tinting technique allows you to match or accent bare wood or stain while leveling wood pores. For step-by-step instructions, see pages 54–55.*

A Brush-up Course

From newly available water-based varnish and paint strippers to multicolor sponging techniques, this updated version of *Furniture Finishing* offers the latest discoveries in materials and methods.

Whether you're providing new life for a family heirloom or giving an adventuresome lift to a flea-market find, we present all the information you need to choose the appropriate tools for the job. With step-by-step photos and art, we also show you exactly how to bring your project to fruition.

Many professionals, amateur refinishers, and designers shared their knowledge with us and allowed us to photograph their creations. We'd especially like to thank Creative Paint & Wallpaper, George V Collection of San Francisco, Rick Ricardo of Showplace Antiques, and The Woodsmith.

Special thanks also go to Marcia Morrill Williamson for carefully editing the manuscript, to JoAnn Masaoka Van Atta for scouting and styling many of the photographs, and to N. E. Larkin for her help in creating the section on decorative finishes.

Book Editor
Scott Atkinson

Coordinating Editor
Suzanne Normand Eyre

Design
Joe di Chiarro

Illustrations
Lois Lovejoy

Cover: A coat of varnish goes atop a freshly stripped and stained chair. Cover design by Scott Atkinson and Susan Bryant. Photography by Philip Harvey. Photo styling by JoAnn Masaoka Van Atta. Chair courtesy of Fenton MacLaren of Berkeley.

Photographers: **Scott Atkinson:** 21 bottom left, 21 bottom right center; **Glenn Christiansen:** 73 top left; **Philip Harvey:** 2, 4, 5, 6, 8, 9, 12, 13, 18, 21 top left center, 26, 36, 39, 52 bottom, 63 top right, 67, 71, 73 bottom right, 76, 78, 80, 81 bottom, 88 top, 89 top; **Ells Marugg:** 21 top left, 21 bottom left center, 21 top right center, 21 right, 66, 72 top left, 75; **Norman A. Plate:** 92; **Tom Wyatt:** 1, 24, 25, 42, 43, 44, 46, 47, 48, 49, 50, 51, 52 top left, 52 top middle, 52 top right, 53, 54, 55, 56, 62, 63 bottom left, 64, 65, 68, 69, 70, 72 bottom right, 74, 81 top left, 81 top right, 82, 83, 84, 85, 86, 87, 88 bottom left, 88 center, 88 right, 89 bottom left, 89 bottom center, 89 bottom right, 90, 93, 94, 95.

Editor: Elizabeth L. Hogan

First printing May 1992

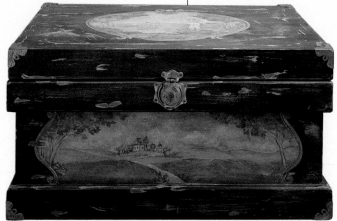

DECORATIVE PAINTING: CROWORKS OF MARIN

Multiple layers *of color were brushed onto chest, then worn down by sanding. For additional antiquing ideas and techniques, see pages 80–83.*

Contents

What Are Your Options?

Many homes harbor one or more furniture pieces that could be given a new lease on life by a fresh surface treatment. And many people, either challenged by a raw piece of unfinished new furniture or confronting a fading antique, find they want to learn more about finishing or refinishing wood furniture.

You probably have this book in hand because you feel a certain piece of furniture needs help. But before you jump in, you need to think out your approach.

Respect Your Elders

Save yourself time and effort on any refinishing job by deciding whether or not the old finish must be totally removed. In many cases that's not necessary (see "Can This Finish Be Saved?" on pages 20–22). Often all an old finish needs is a good cleaning or, at most, a speedily accomplished facelift.

Another question to consider from the beginning is whether you prefer a rich old patina or a new-wood look. "Patina" is a darkening of the wood surface brought about by changes in the atmosphere and by the aging process itself. This delicate coloring — the product of perhaps a century or more — adds to the value of an antique, distinguishing a truly lovely old piece from a modern reproduction or an outright impostor.

If the old finish can't be saved or rejuvenated, it will have to come off before refinishing can begin. You'll find detailed advice on pages 23–25.

Artist's acrylics

DECORATIVE ARTIST: N. E. LARKIN

Hand-rubbed beeswax

What about wobbly table legs or flapping drawers? We've included a primer on repairs: see pages 27–35. Take care of these nicks and scrapes first, because once you begin applying the finish, it's difficult to go back and reglue something you missed.

Starting From Scratch

If the furniture is new, you can skip pages 18–35, which deal specifically with refinishing. But before you pick up your paintbrush, allow time for careful wood preparation. Even new, unfinished furniture is likely to require additional smoothing. See pages 37–43 for instructions.

Then, too, you might want to stain the piece for color flair or camouflage, or to fill wood pores with matching or contrasting color. Pages 45–55, "Coloring Your Project," take up these possibilities.

Do you want a penetrating finish, a clear surface finish, or colorful enamel? Pages 8–11 spell out the options. When you're ready to brush or spray, you'll find illustrated step-by-step help in Chapter 5, "Applying the Final Finish."

Decorative Options

Of course, applying a clear finish is not the only way to enhance and protect unfinished or discarded furniture. Decorative finishes (paint, two-tone glazes, gilding, even varnished paper collage) can be applied over bare wood or an old finish. In fact, if your piece is of marginal quality or construction, an opaque finish may be the only answer.

Making wood look "old" is easy (especially on new, unfinished pieces), and may be necessary if an heirloom's original patina has been badly damaged. In Chapter 6, "Special Decorative Finishes," we offer plenty of ideas for imparting a look of time-honored style, using techniques such as pickling, antiquing, and distressing. You'll also find ideas for other decorative tricks, from traditional stenciling to colorful sponging and marbling — and more.

Antique glazing

High-gloss lacquer

DESIGN: FLEGEL'S HOME FURNISHINGS

DECORATIVE PAINTING: CROWORKS OF MARIN

Tools
&
Materials

Before jumping too quickly into the finishing or refinishing process, you need to be sure you understand the nature of the tools and materials involved. This chapter is a good starting place: it presents the basic finishing options, reviews the use of brushes and other tools, and provides a primer on common furniture woods.

A trip to any paint or hardware store will reveal a wide range of wood-finishing products, and new chemical combinations keep expanding that list. First, you have to decide whether or not to use a stain — and if so, which one. Then comes choosing a protective coating, either clear or enamel. The chart on page 10 will help you assess the possibilities.

The quality of your tools goes a long way toward determining the outcome — and the "hassle factor"— of your project. Generally, furniture finishing is not a tool-intensive endeavor; but power sanders, spray guns, and other modern accessories can sometimes make the going much easier.

Are you a little confused about just what distinguishes one wood type from another? We offer a crash course in basic wood terminology, explain sheet materials and veneers, provide photos and descriptions of species used in furniture, and suggest appropriate finishes.

If you have trouble finding any particular wood-finishing supplies in your area, consult the list of mail-order sources on page 14.

*A **huge array of products** — including colorful stains, easy-to-use clear finishes, enamels, and custom tinting agents — awaits today's furniture finisher. Locate supplies at paint stores, hardware stores, arts and crafts outlets, or through mail-order sources.*

Finishing Options

A fine finish protects wood from dirt, abrasion, moisture, heat, and chemicals. It can also enhance both the appearance and the "feel" of the wood. You can choose from two types of clear finish — those that penetrate wood pores and those that are built up in layers on top of the surface. You might also choose to apply additional color — subtle or bold — in the form of a stain or enamel. Here's a look at the basic options; you'll find additional details in Chapter 4, "Coloring Your Project," and Chapter 5, "Applying the Final Finish."

For any piece of furniture, there may be two or three finishes that seem desirable. Choosing the one that meets your needs best often means weighing various factors. Consider the following:

■ *Appearance.* Think about texture, color, and gloss (sheen). Some finishes make the surface glassy-smooth; others emphasize wood pores and grain. One stain might complement a certain piece; another might hide the natural beauty of the wood's color and pattern.

■ *Application.* Some finishes are simply spread onto the wood, leaving the furniture ready for use in a few hours. Others must be applied in several coats and demand much rubbing between coats. Don't automatically choose the low road: many furniture finishers believe that you get what you pay for, in time and effort as well as in quality of materials.

■ *Compatibility.* If you're planning a clear finish over bare, unfinished wood, your choices are broad. But if you're staining, filling, sealing, and/or refinishing a previously finished piece, you must be sure all products are compatible. Otherwise, the layers won't bond, and your achievement will be short-lived.

■ *Durability.* Any finish you select for your furniture is fine, so long as it pleases you. But if your newly finished piece is subject to constant wear or to abuse from children and pets, or if you do a lot of entertaining, you'll want to create a surface that will withstand rough treatment as it protects the wood.

What's your choice: brash color, a natural look, or a glossy surface finish? Examples of each are shown here. Sea-blue dye stain adds punch to modern chair (left); aged pine hutch (center) has hand-rubbed wax finish; French-polished rosewood table (far right) shines with shellac.

■ *Upkeep.* Beware! Some finishes require more intensive maintenance than others — waxing, polishing, repairing scratches, and just keeping off dust and dirt.

Stains

Stain is probably the most misunderstood and misused material in wood finishing. Many woods, especially dark, highly figured species, have beautiful natural color that requires no stain at all. But when used on light-colored, nondescript wood, stain can add some color and a bit of character and can also highlight the grain. Staining is sometimes an effective way to make one wood species resemble another or to blend new and old materials.

In most cases, stains are not final finishes; they're for color or accent only. You still need to protect the surface of your piece by sealing it with a clear finish.

Although you may encounter many stain names and brands in the market, products really fall into two general types: *pigmented stains* and *dyes*.

Pigmented stains, sold as oil stain, wood stain, and pigmented wiping stain, are composed of finely ground particles of color held in suspension in oil or

DESIGN: AGNES BOURNE

solvent. Essentially a thin paint, this type of stain lodges in pores and other spaces between wood fibers. These stains tend to conceal the grain, so some professionals don't like them. But they are the most commonly available choices in retail stores. They're easy to apply (see pages 48–49) with a brush or rag.

Most wood dyes are aniline (a coal-tar derivative), dissolved in various substances. These dyes are actually absorbed by the wood fibers and so allow the grain to show through. In addition to wood tones, you'll find brilliant colors — wine red, blue, yellow, even bright green. Dye stains can be hard to find at retail outlets; shop at a woodworking or wood-finishing specialty store or try one of the mail-order sources listed on page 14.

Six basic stain categories are discussed on page 10. Remember, though, that the modern tendency to market "one-step" products has resulted in stain/filler combinations, pigmented sealers, and all-in-one stain finishes — as well as pigment/dye blends. Many of these products work well. Though they give you less control over each step, they also eliminate some of the trouble.

Clear Finishes

It will simplify your finishing decision to know that all clear finishing products generally fall into two basic types: penetrating finishes and surface coatings. Other wood finishes are often only variations of these.

Because many finishes are not easily categorized, it's important to read labels carefully. Examining the list of solids, which will be primarily resins and oils, will help you determine the finish's type. If you're still in doubt, ask your paint dealer for advice. Comparing notes with other woodworkers is also an excellent way of identifying a reliable finish.

Penetrating finishes. These soak into the wood pores to give furniture a natural look and feel. Though a penetrating finish sinks below the wood's surface, it is still fairly durable and can often resist stains, chemicals, and liquids without the "dipped-in-plastic" look of some more protective coatings, such as polyurethane.

Natural and synthetic oils and resins are the most popular penetrating finishes. The natural ones — such

A LOOK AT FINISHING PRODUCTS

STAINS

Pigmented oil stain	Simple to apply; won't fade or bleed. Useful for making one wood species look like another. Heavy pigments tend to obscure grain and gum up pores in hardwoods such as oak and walnut. Not compatible with shellac or lacquer.
Penetrating oil stain	One-step product stains with dyes rather than pigments, so pores and grain show through. Similar to penetrating resin, but with color added. Produces irregular results on softwoods and plywoods. Handy for repairs, touch-up jobs.
Gel stain	May contain both pigments and dyes. Very easy to apply (just wipe on and let dry), but results may be uneven on large surfaces.
Water-based aniline dye	Colors are brilliant, clear, and permanent. Since water raises wood grain, resanding is necessary. Very slow drying. Sold in powdered form; may be hard to find.
Alcohol-based aniline dye	Quick-drying alcohol stains won't raise grain, but aren't very light-fast; best reserved for small touch-up jobs. Should be sprayed on to avoid lap marks.
Non-grain-raising (NGR) **stain**	Bright, transparent colors; won't raise wood grain. Available premixed by mail. Very short drying time; best when sprayed. Not for use on softwoods.

PENETRATING FINISHES

Boiled linseed oil	Lends warm, slightly dull patina to wood. Dries very slowly and requires many coats. Moderate resistance to heat, water, and chemicals. Easily renewable.
Tung oil	Natural oil finish that's hard and highly resistant to abrasion, moisture, heat, acid, and mildew. Requires several thin, hand-rubbed applications (heavy coats wrinkle badly). Best with polymer resins added.
Penetrating resin (Danish oil, antique oil)	Use on hard, open-grain woods. Leaves wood looking and feeling "natural." Easy to apply and retouch but doesn't protect against heat or abrasion. May darken some woods.
Rub-on varnish	Penetrating resin and varnish combination that builds up sheen as coats are applied; dries fairly quickly. Moderately resistant to water and alcohol; darkens wood.

SURFACE FINISHES

Shellac	Lends warm luster to wood. Easy to apply, retouch, and remove. Excellent sealer. Lays down in thin, quick-drying coats that can be rubbed to a high sheen. Little resistance to heat, alcohol, and moisture. Comes in white (blonde), orange, and brownish (button) versions. Available in flake form or premixed.
Lacquer (nitrocellulose)	Strong, clear, quick-drying finish in both spraying and brushing form; very durable, though vulnerable to moisture. Requires 3 or more coats; can be polished to a high gloss. Noxious fumes; highly flammable.
Lacquer (water-based)	Easier to clean, less toxic, and much less flammable than nitrocellulose—a more practical spray product for do-it-yourselfer. Raises grain; use sanding sealer. May dry more slowly than nitrocellulose lacquer. Can smell strongly of ammonia.
Alkyd varnish	Widely compatible oil-based interior varnish that produces a thick coating with good overall resistance. Dries slowly and darkens with time. Brush marks and dust can be a problem.
Phenolic-resin varnish (spar varnish)	Tough, exterior varnish with excellent weathering resistance; flexes with wood's seasonal changes. To avoid yellowing, product should contain ultraviolet absorbers.
Polyurethane varnish	Thick, plastic, irreversible coating that's nearly impervious to water, heat, and alcohol. Dries overnight. Incompatible with some stains and sealers. Follow instructions to ensure good bonding between coats.
Water-based varnish	Easy cleanup. Dries quickly. Nontoxic when dry. Although early versions lacked durability, new products are greatly improved. Finish goes on milky, but dries clear and won't yellow. Raises wood grain. May require numerous coats. Expensive.
Enamel	Available in flat, semigloss, and gloss finishes, and in a wide range of colors. May have lacquer or varnish (alkyd, polyurethane, or water) base; each shares same qualities as clear finish of the same type.
Wax	Occasionally used as a finish, especially on antiques or "aged" pine. More often applied over harder top coats. Increases luster of wood. Not very durable, but offers some protection against liquids when renewed frequently. Available in various shades.

as linseed oil — have played a major role in furniture finishing. Today, however, tung oils, penetrating resins, and rub-on varnishes are more popular because they are as beautiful as natural oil but easier to use.

Surface coatings. These lie on top of the wood and provide protection in the form of a thin, durable shield. This kind of coating, often available in a number of sheens, is glasslike in appearance but can be dulled down by any of a variety of methods if desired. When properly maintained, a good surface finish will make your furniture relatively safe from dropped objects, scratches, stains, chemicals, heat, and other potential damagers.

Shellac is the classic natural surface finish, associated with fine furniture for hundreds of years. Warmtoned and subtle, it's easy to apply, quick-drying, and can be built up with complete assurance because the alcohol in each new coat softens the previous coat (no matter how old) and bonds the two. On the other hand, shellac's alcohol content makes this finish vulnerable to a spilled cocktail, strong soaps, and detergents. And shellac can't take much heat or moisture: it turns cloudy.

Lacquer, another so-called "evaporative" finish, is similar to shellac, but harder and more durable. It can be rubbed to a high sheen. Even with these advantages, though, lacquer is seldom the choice of the do-it-yourself finisher because it dries extremely quickly and is difficult to apply successfully without spray equipment. Special brushing lacquers can be purchased, however; these are discussed on pages 70–71.

Varnish is an excellent choice for a durable surface finish. Traditional varnishes were first developed by mixing linseed oil with shellac. Most modern synthetic finishes, as well as plastic finishes and polyurethanes, are elaborations of this original formula. Varnish is a "reactive" finish, requiring sanding or scuffing for top coats to adhere; polyurethane is particularly unforgiving in this respect. The reactive process is generally a slow one, providing an opening for varnish's number one nemesis: dust.

Environmental concerns are fostering development of a new generation of nontoxic, water-based varnishes and lacquers. The key phrase is "volatile organic compounds" (VOCs) — the amount of air-polluting solvents in traditional finishing products. Government regulations restricting VOCs have already been passed in numerous states, and it seems likely that these regulations will be the rule, not the exception, within a few years.

VOC content is certainly not the only good news about these new formulations. In addition to improved hardness and durability (problems with earlier products), today's water-based varnishes boast easy cleanup, accelerated drying times, and superior clarity (they don't go yellowish) to traditional varnishes. There are problems: these products raise wood grain, are susceptible to humidity and temperature during application, and have a disturbing milky whiteness (though they dry quite clear). Harder-to-find water-based lacquers offer the home finisher another plus: you can spray them on furniture without constructing a special spray booth.

Enamel Paints

The most common types for interior surfaces are water-based (latex) enamels and oil-based (alkyd) enamels. Since there's no industry standard for sheens, a medium gloss may be called pearl, semigloss, or some other name, and it can range from moderately to very shiny, depending on the manufacturer. The glossier the finish, the more durable and washable it is. A finish with a sheen is referred to as an enamel finish.

Other paints — including colored lacquers, artist's acrylics, japan colors, universal colors, and traditional milk paints — are handy for creating decorative finishes, tinting stains and varnish, or making spot repairs.

Latex (water-based) paints. Latexes account for the vast majority of paint sold today, and with good reason. Because water is their solvent, latex paints dry quickly — usually in a little more than an hour, although a full cure can take up to 2 weeks. Also, latex paints are practically odorless. Best of all, you can clean up with soap and water.

On the down side, although today's latex high-gloss finishes are as shiny as alkyd ones, they're not as durable. Also, unlike an alkyd finish, latex tears or becomes gummy when you try to sand it.

You can tell latex quality by the type of resin used. The best and most durable latex paint contains 100 percent acrylic resin. Vinyl acrylic and other blends are next in quality. A latex paint containing only vinyl resin is least durable.

Alkyd paints. These oil-based paints, made of synthetic resins, have largely replaced paints containing linseed and other natural oils. Alkyds are more durable than latex paints and generally level out better, drying virtually free of brush marks. They have "bite," a sticking quality not inherent in latex. You can sand an alkyd surface easily — a critical factor if you're applying successive coats.

On the other hand, alkyds are harder to apply, tend to sag more, and take longer to dry. Alkyds require cleanup with paint thinner.

Safety goggles

Rubber gloves

Painter's mask

⚠ WARNING

Foam brushes

Pad applicator

Respirator

3-inch-wide roller

Synthetic-filament brush

3" = 76.2 ᵐ/ₘ

HVLP spray gun

Natural-bristle brush

ools of the Trade

Even the best finishing products can yield disappointing results if you don't have the right equipment. High-quality brushes and other tools that are appropriate for the particular task and used correctly will help you achieve a professional-looking job.

For a look at some basic finishing and safety gear, see the facing page. For information on tools for repairing or preparing wood, see chapters 2 and 3. Decorative finishes may require their own arsenal of paraphernalia: combs, stippling brushes, sponges, feathers, even chains and car keys. For details, see Chapter 6, "Special Decorative Techniques."

Choosing a Brush

The best brush you can afford, properly cared for, is actually the most economical choice. Since it is nearly impossible to do a good finishing job with a poor-quality brush, consider the following points when you shop for brushes.

Natural-bristle brushes are traditionally used to apply alkyd varnish and other finishes that clean up in paint thinner. Don't use them for applying latex and other water-based products: the bristles become limp when they soak up water.

Choose a synthetic-filament brush for water-based finishes. Polyester bristles stay sturdy in water, keeping their shape for detail work. A well-made synthetic brush can also be used with alkyd materials.

Good-quality brushes perform very differently from lesser ones. A good brush is balanced, holds a lot of finish, and puts the finish where you want it. For an illustration of what to look for, compare the brushes pictured above right.

The bristles should be thick, flexible, and tapered so that they're thicker at the base than at the tip; and they should be set firmly into the handle with epoxy cement, not glue. Bounce the brush against the back of your hand. Good bristles feel soft and silky, and they spread evenly when you apply pressure.

Fan out the bristles and check for flags, or split ends. The more flags there are, the more finish the brush can hold. Most of the bristles should be long, but you should find some short bristles mixed among the longer ones.

For woodworking, stick with brushes that are from 1 to 3 inches wide. The 1-inch brush is good for edges and delicate trim; use a 2- or 3-inch version for large, flat surfaces. Rounded varnish brushes flow well and offer good edge control but are expensive.

BRUSH COMPARISON

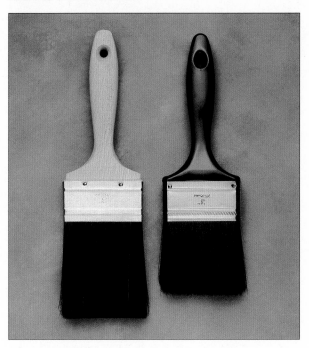

Superior-quality brush (at left) has long, flagged bristles firmly set into an easy-to-grip wood handle. On less expensive brush (at right), bristles are short and splayed, connection isn't as secure, and plastic handle may feel slippery during use.

Brush Alternatives

A 3-inch-wide paint roller can apply enamel quickly and smoothly to large surfaces. Choose a roller cover appropriate for the finish you're using. With water-based materials, you'll want a nylon cover. For alkyd paint, choose a nylon-and-wool blend, lambskin, or mohair cover. Nap thickness on roller covers varies from $\frac{1}{16}$ inch to 1¼ inches. The smoother the surface you're painting, the shorter the nap you'll need.

A pad applicator, which resembles a sponge attached to a short handle, is even simpler to use. As with roller covers made of the same materials, nylon pads are used with latex paints. Nylon-and-wool, lambskin, and mohair pads are best for alkyds. If cleanup isn't your strong suit, look for disposable foam brushes; they produce similar results and are very useful for laying on stains and oil finishes.

Spray Units

By far the fastest method of applying a wood finish is with a spray gun. A traditional pressurized spray system consists of a spray gun that holds and distributes the finishing material, an air compressor (either gasoline-powered or electric) that provides the propellant

MAIL-ORDER SOURCES

As you become more adept at repairing and finishing furniture, you may need more specialized wood-finishing tools and supplies. Such supplies are seldom stocked in neighborhood paint or hardware stores because there is relatively little demand for them.

If you cannot find water stains, padding lacquers, shellac sticks, or any other wood-finishing material or tool mentioned in this book, here are a few mail-order firms that can help you. Call or write for their catalogs. The yellow pages of your telephone directory can also help you locate antique and unfinished furniture, spray lacquer and spray guns, or sheet materials and hardwoods.

Sources for Woodworking Supplies

Albert Constantine and Son, Inc.
2050 Eastchester Rd.
Bronx, NY 10461
800-223-8087

Brookstone
Vose Farm Rd.
Peterborough, NH 03458
603-924-7181

Garrett Wade Company, Inc.
161 Avenue of the Americas
New York, NY 10013
800-221-2942 (orders)
212-807-1155 (customer service)

Mohawk Finishing Products, Inc.
Route 30 North
Amsterdam, NY 12010
518-843-1380

Sears, Roebuck & Company
800-366-3000

Woodcraft Supply Corp.
210 Wood County Industrial Park
Dept. 91WW09H
P.O. Box 1686
Parkersburg, WV 26101-1686
800-542-9115

The Woodworker's Store
21801 Industrial Blvd.
Rogers, MN 55374
612-428-2899 or 612-428-2199 (orders)

Woodworker's Supply, Inc.
5604 Alameda Place NE
Albuquerque, NM 87113
800-645-9292

Sources for Oil Glazes

Liberty Paint Corp.
969 Columbia St.
Hudson, NY 12534
518-828-4060

McCloskey Co.
Benjamin Moore & Co.
Pratt & Lambert, Inc.
(See yellow pages under Paint)

Sources for Acrylic Glazes

Cal-Western Paints, Inc.
11748 Slauson Ave.
Santa Fe Springs, CA 90670
310-693-0872

Janovic Plaza
1150 Third Ave.
New York, NY 10021
212-772-1400

Liberty Paint Corp.
969 Columbia St.
Hudson, NY 12534
518-828-4060

for the gun, and (in some cases) a holding tank to equalize and store the compressed air until needed.

A recent boon for both the small shop and home refinisher comes in the form of so-called HVLP spray units. As the letters indicate, these guns deliver a higher volume of finish at lower pressure than do standard guns. Major advantages of HVLP units include far less misting than with standard guns, less overspray, and less bounceback. Not only will these compact, portable units save you money on finish, they're better for the environment, too. Their turbines operate on 120-volt household current.

Whichever gun type you choose, if you're spraying water-based finishing materials, you'll want to be sure the internal parts are of stainless steel to prevent rusting. If you choose not to purchase your own spray equipment, you can usually rent a spray gun and accessories at a paint store or tool rental shop.

Inexpensive airless or electric sprayers are also available, but beware: sometimes their output is not significantly greater than that of an aerosol can.

Safety Gear

Personal accessories designed to protect you from injury should be considered essential equipment. Here's a basic outfit. For tips on setting up a safe, efficient work area, see page 23.

Respirator or painter's mask. You must protect against inhaling harmful fumes, mist, or dust; the finer the vapors, the better the respirator you'll need. Interchangeable filters are rated for special requirements. For most finishing, you'll want chemical cartridges intended for organic vapors, dusts, and mists.

Inexpensive, disposable painter's masks screen out heavy sawdust and some mists. They're handy for prep work and for applying some finishes in tight quarters. However, when fumes or fine mists are involved, they're no substitute for a good respirator.

Work gloves. Whenever you're working with finishing materials, solvents, or adhesives, wear rubber or plastic gloves. They protect you from excess skin absorption and also make cleanup a lot easier — just peel them off. Dishwashing or medical examination gloves are fine for most work; thicker "refinisher's gloves" are designed for handling chemical strippers.

Safety goggles. These are a must when operating power tools and high-impact hand tools. They're also handy for working with finishing materials in a cramped area. Look for a pair that fits comfortably and won't fog unduly — otherwise, you probably won't wear them.

now Your Woods

Furniture woods vary widely in color, pore size, figure, strength, and workability. They also accept finishing products and treatments in different ways. You'll want to know the properties of the type of wood you're working with before you begin any project.

Lumber Lingo: A Crash Course

A working knowledge of wood terms and distinctions can help you navigate the antique shop, bare-furniture warehouse, or paint store more efficiently.

Lumber is divided into *hardwoods* and *softwoods*, terms that refer to the origin of the wood. Hardwoods come from deciduous trees, softwoods from conifers. Generally, softwoods are less expensive, easier to cut and shape, and less figured than hardwoods. But hardwoods tend to take stains and finishes better, provide more varied color and grain, and resist wear better.

The terms below should help to explain some other common lumber distinctions.

Heartwood is the wood extending from the soft core of the tree (pith) to the sapwood (wood tissue of pale coloring near the outside of the tree). Besides color differences, heartwood is generally of better quality.

Grain and *figure* are the natural design and pattern in wood, and are affected by the way the wood is cut. Flat-sawn wood is cut at a tangent to the growth rings; it's usually the least expensive cut. Quarter-sawn wood is cut nearly perpendicular to the growth rings; it's also called "vertical-grain." Rift-sawn pieces are similar to quarter-sawn, but cut at about 45° to the growth rings.

Grain, figure, and the size and distribution of wood pores determine the wood's texture. Some species are naturally hard and smooth; others have large pores that must be filled if you want a smooth feel in the finished piece.

Besides solid lumber, sheet products are increasingly used in furniture. Plywood is manufactured lumber, made of thin wood layers glued together. Fiberboard and particle board, two other contemporary standbys, are made from particles of wood impregnated with glue and pressed into sheets. Raw particle board has a speckled appearance.

Many types of hardwood are available in thin veneers. These flexible sheets, 1/16 inch thick or even thinner, are used to dress up plywood, particle board, and inexpensive grades of wood. Unless you're careful, it's easy to sand through veneers or to loosen them with excess finish or chemical stripper. To determine whether a surface is veneer, look for seams at edges and ends; or check interior parts for the telltale core material.

A Guide to Wood Species

The photographs on pages 16–17 show a selection of popular furniture woods. For identification, match the photographed wood against such details of your furniture's wood as its pores, its characteristic grain pattern, and the color of its surface. Then read on to learn more about the particular wood's properties, range of growth, and common uses — and the finishing methods recommended for it.

In some cases, true wood characteristics may be camouflaged by pigmented stains, fillers, or semi-opaque finishes. Try to be sure your wood is free from these disguises before you attempt to identify it.

LUMBER DETAILS

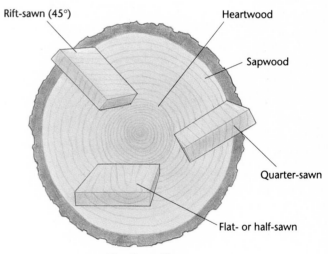

Hardwood log

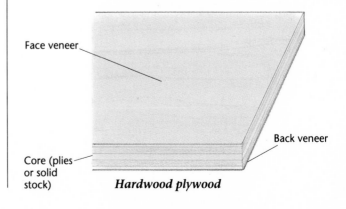

Hardwood plywood

A Guide to Wood Species

Ash, white

Source: Eastern and Southern states. *Color and pattern:* Creamy white to grayish brown. Prominent, wide grain. Open pores. *Characteristics:* Tough and heavy with good shock resistance; used for baseball bats and tool handles. *Finish:* Clear finish over bare wood or over light or dark stain.

Beech, American

Source: Great Lake and Mid-Atlantic states. *Color and pattern:* Reddish brown heartwood and creamy white sapwood. Conspicuous wood rays. Virtually invisible pores. *Characteristics:* Heavy and hard, but prone to checking and warping. Imparts no odor or taste to kitchen items. *Finish:* Clear finish over bare wood or stain.

Birch, yellow

Source: Great Lake and Eastern states, Canada. *Color and pattern:* Creamy white to light reddish brown. Wavy grain. Extremely small pores. *Characteristics:* Hard, heavy, and strong. Somewhat unstable (it warps), but the favorite plywood of many cabinetmakers. *Finish:* Clear finish over bare wood or over light or dark stain. Birch plywood takes enamel very well.

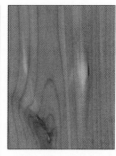

Cedar, Eastern red

Source: Southeastern and South Central states; several related Western species as well. *Color and pattern:* Light red heartwood with ivory-colored sapwood streaks throughout. Knotty pattern and other natural markings always present. *Characteristics:* Highly aromatic and moderately hard, though brittle. *Finish:* Unfinished, or only a thin, clear finish over bare wood.

Cherry, black

Source: Eastern states and Canada. *Color and pattern:* Light to dark reddish brown. Straight grain. Small, individual pores. *Characteristics:* Moderately hard and stable, but not heavy. Works easily and takes a satiny finish. Absolute favorite of many woodworkers. *Finish:* Clear finish over bare wood or light (frequently reddish) stain.

Pecan

Source: Southern states. *Color and pattern:* Creamy white to reddish brown. Uniform grain, with occasional dark streaks. Large pores. *Characteristics:* Very heavy, hard, and strong. Must be seasoned carefully. Easily worked. *Finish:* Clear finish over bare wood or over light or dark stain.

Pine, white

Source: From the East comes Eastern white pine; from the West come white pine, sugar pine, and (most popular) ponderosa pine. *Color and pattern:* Cream to light reddish brown. Visible resin canals and obvious growth rings. *Characteristics:* Moderately light, soft. *Finish:* Clear finish over bare wood or over light or dark stain. Seal before staining. Often enameled.

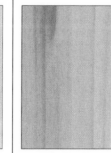

Poplar, yellow

Source: Eastern states, Southeastern Canada. *Color and pattern:* Light yellow to brownish yellow with a greenish tinge. Even texture and straight grain pattern. Barely visible pores. *Characteristics:* The "pine" of hardwoods: medium to light in weight and moderately soft. *Finish:* Clear finish over light or dark stain. Often enameled.

Redwood

Source: California and Oregon. *Color and pattern:* Deep reddish brown heartwood; sapwood is lighter. Obvious alternating glossy and mat growth rings. *Characteristics:* Medium to light in weight. Moderately soft. Resists decay and termites. *Finish:* Clear finish over bare wood.

Elm, American

Source: Eastern states.
Color and pattern: Light brown to dark brown, often containing shades of red. Straight grain pattern with obvious light and dark boundaries. *Characteristics:* Moderately hard and heavy. Excellent bending qualities. *Finish:* Clear finish over light or dark stain.

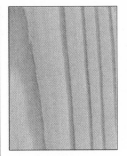

Fir, Douglas

Source: Pacific and Rocky Mountain states. *Color and pattern:* Creamy white to yellowish. *Characteristics:* Moderately heavy, hard, and stiff. Quarter-sawn "vertical-grain" fir has beautiful straight grain. *Finish:* Clear finish over bare wood or over light or dark stain (use sealer before staining). Sometimes painted.

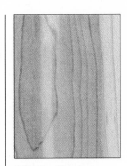

Mahogany

Source: Central America and Africa. *Color and pattern:* Golden through reddish brown to dark red. Often a highly figured grain pattern. Open pores. *Characteristics:* Moderately hard, even-textured, and heavy. (Philippine mahogany, another species, is comparatively soft.) *Finish:* Clear finish over bare wood, or over a light stain (reddish dyes popular).

Maple, Eastern

Source: Great Lake and Eastern states. *Color and pattern:* Creamy white to light reddish brown. Great variety in grain (including curly and bird's-eye types). *Characteristics:* Heavy, hard, and strong. Easy to work. *Finish:* Clear finish over bare wood or over light stain. Orange shellac or tinted lacquer can add color to cool-toned maple.

Oak

Source: Eastern and Midwestern states. *Color and pattern:* Light grayish brown to reddish brown. Striking grain figure. Large, open pores. White oak has distinctive light rays when quarter-sawn. *Characteristics:* Heavy, hard, and very wear resistant. *Finish:* Takes clear finish and stain beautifully, especially penetrating types. Requires filler to create a smooth surface.

Rosewood

Source: Brazil, Southern India and Ceylon. *Color and pattern:* Various shades of dark brown to dark purple. Conspicuous black streaks. Large, open pores. *Characteristics:* Very heavy, very hard, and oily, with a coarse texture. All types finish beautifully. *Finish:* Clear finish over bare wood.

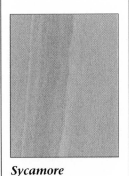

Sycamore

Source: Eastern and Southern states. *Color and pattern:* Pale reddish brown. Obvious wide growth pattern. Small pores. *Characteristics:* Moderately heavy and hard. Fine-textured, with good shock resistance. *Finish:* Clear finish over bare wood or over stain.

Teak

Source: Burma, Java, Thailand. *Color and pattern:* Tawny yellow to dark brown. Frequent lighter and darker streaks. Pattern very similar to that of walnut. *Characteristics:* Heavy, strong, oily, and tough; eats saw blades. *Finish:* Clear finish (usually penetrating type) over bare wood.

Walnut, black

Source: Central and Eastern states, Canada. *Color and pattern:* Light gray-brown to dark purple-brown and chocolates. Wide variety of plain and highly figured patterns. Fine texture. *Characteristics:* Hard as nails, moderately heavy, and stiff. Takes a high polish. *Finish:* Clear finish over bare wood. Can be bleached or lightly stained.

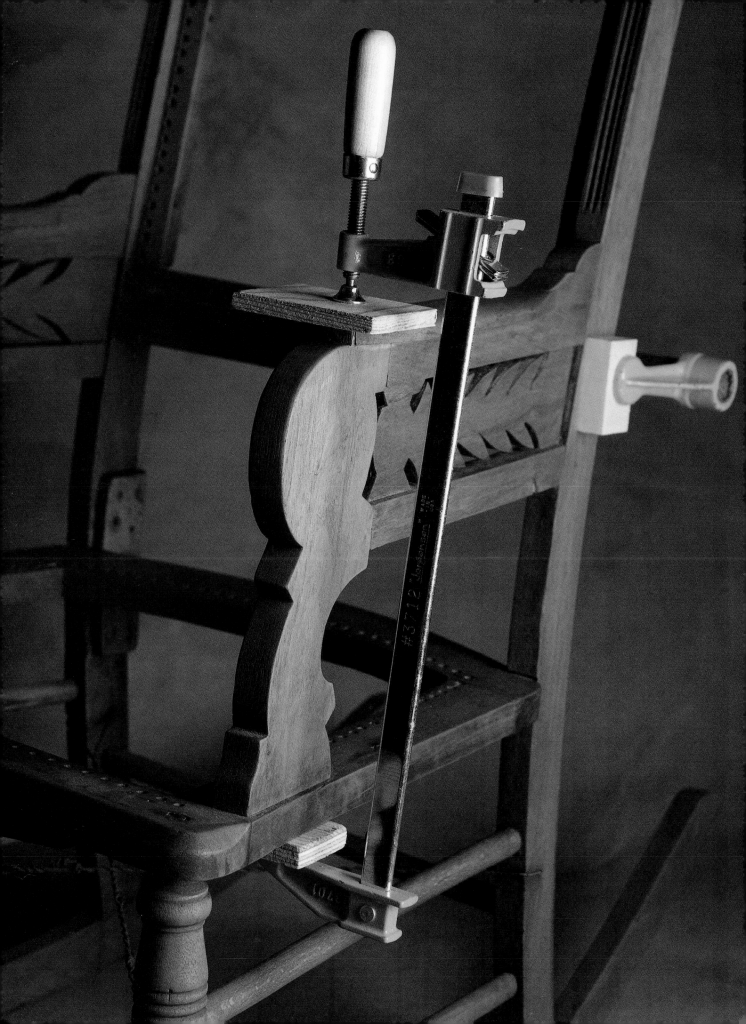

Stripping & Repairs

Before you apply any new finish to an existing piece of furniture, make sure the piece is ready to receive that finish. The furniture must be structurally solid and ready for many more years of use, and the surface of the wood must be smooth and clean so the new finish will go on unblemished.

But consider your options. Complete finish removal is not always necessary — nor is it advisable on very early antiques. Unless the previous finish has been badly damaged or allowed to weather, it can often be saved with a minimum of restoration.

On the other hand, if the existing finish is in obviously poor condition or if you're planning to add a new stain, you'll probably need to strip the piece to bare wood.

Any structural damage that is not repaired will only shorten the life of the newly refinished furniture once it's put into use. Surface blemishes that may seem to be hardly worth repairing will be emphasized and intensified when you apply a stain and a final clear finish to the wood. For this reason, you should evaluate minor as well as major damage.

Remember, though, that the charm of old furniture is sometimes related to visible signs of its age and use. You may want to honor those marks!

Many furniture repairs are not difficult to make if you have patience and a few basic tools. This chair, suffering from loose joints and past "quickie" repairs, is gaining a new lease on life through careful regluing; bar and pipe clamps apply the pressure.

Can This Finish Be Saved?

Sometimes old furniture that appears to need refinishing can be restored simply by repairing the original finish. When this is possible, you can preserve the authentic quality of the furniture and at the same time save yourself effort and energy.

Preliminary Cleaning

You may find that all a piece needs to bring it back to life is a little cleaning. Even if more extensive repair will be required, this is the first step.

Start with a mild solution of soap and water and rub gently along the grain. For extra clout, try a little trisodium phosphate (TSP), but not too much: heavy concentrations can eat through some finishes.

To remove a heavy buildup of old wax, clean the wood with a rag lightly moistened with paint thinner or turpentine.

If cleaning is successful, all you'll need is a coat of paste wax (pages 74–75) to restore the original sheen.

Five Alternatives to Refinishing

Regardless of the type of finishing defect on your furniture, most damage can easily be repaired. The methods described here are listed in order of increasing difficulty. Be sure to test your hand in an inconspicuous place before you start working on more visible areas.

Determine what the old finish is so you can have some idea of how to repair it. Most pre-1920s clear finishes contain shellac and are dissolvable in denatured alcohol. Nearly all commercial furniture made after 1920 has been sprayed with lacquer, which dissolves in lacquer thinner. Varnish won't dissolve, but it should crack and rise if exposed to lacquer thinner or paint removers.

Abrasion. A shellac, lacquer, or varnish finish is often 1/50 to 1/30 inch thick and very tough. Sometimes a finish is so tough that blemishes, such as white spots or water rings, only penetrate through the top 5 percent of the surface coat. The technique of abrasion wears away this damaged layer to reveal the healthy 95 percent of the finish underneath.

Prepare the surface of your piece for light abrasion by cleaning off any wax or oil-based polish that may have built up over the years (see "Preliminary Cleaning," at left).

Next, take part of a pad of 4/0 steel wool (never use an abrasive paper) and dip it lightly in some lubricant — a little paraffin oil, linseed oil, even motor oil. Rub the steel wool back and forth on the surface in the direction of the wood grain. Adjust the pressure of your rubbing to the needs of the situation at hand. As soon as a blemish disappears, stop rubbing; you don't want to rub through the finish to bare wood. When all defects have been removed and the finish looks uniform, wipe off the surface with a dry rag and apply paste wax.

Overcoating. When a finish gets old and thin, there may not be enough left to repair it by the abrasion technique. Overcoating is simply applying a new finish over the remaining serviceable base of the old one.

Begin by cleaning the entire surface. If the original stain has worn through in any areas, retouch these spots with just enough stain (see pages 46–51) to match the surrounding wood.

When the stained areas have thoroughly dried, apply the new finishing coat. Choose any clear finish (shellac, lacquer, or varnish) for the overcoat — as long as it's compatible with the existing finish. If you're

in doubt, test a small amount on some hidden surface of the piece.

When you've completed the overcoating and it has had a chance to dry, wipe the surface with 4/0 steel wool or with a finishing pad. Then apply paste wax.

Reamalgamation. If your furniture has a finish that is only slightly damaged in some way, try the technique of reamalgamation to restore the wood's original beauty. This consists of dissolving and reapplying the finish with the same kind of solvent as was originally used. Reamalgamation is an easy process, and its results are often remarkably successful. Some commercial "furniture refinisher" products are based on the same principle — but cost more.

After cleaning, begin reamalgamating the old finish by dipping a piece of fine steel wool or a flat-bristle brush into the appropriate solvent and applying it to the wood surface. Try to get as much of the surface wet as quickly as possible, before the solvent can evaporate.

Continue brushing or rubbing in the solvent until all the surface defects disappear. Then apply more solvent to the surface and smooth the reamalgamated finish with long, light strokes in the direction of the wood grain. The solvent will dry almost instantly.

When the surface has thoroughly dried, rub it with fresh pieces of 4/0 steel wool or a finishing pad to remove any remaining rough spots. Apply paste wax.

Padding. This term describes the technique of applying a new finish over an old one, using a tightly rolled pad of soft cotton cloth. Though this method is extensively used by professional furniture refinishers, that doesn't mean it is prohibitively difficult. It just takes a little practice.

(Continued on page 22)

TROUBLESHOOTING GUIDE: *Quick Finish Cures*

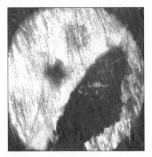

White spots, rings, or cloudiness

Diagnosis: When water penetrates a shellac or lacquer finish, it creates a cloudy, whitish look. If moisture has penetrated through the finish into the wood, the white spots turn black and the problem is much more severe.

Remedy: Since white marks usually occur only in the finish itself, they are often quite easy to repair. Use abrasion for minor problems, reamalgamation for major ones.

Dents

Diagnosis: Dents occur more frequently in softwoods than in hardwoods, but repairs are basically the same for both. The key is to "re-stretch" the compressed wood grain.

Remedy: To remove a dent from unfinished furniture, place a wet cloth over the dent and apply a hot iron over the cloth.

To steam a dent on finished furniture, first puncture the existing finish with small pinholes. Or resort to patching.

Scratches or hairline cracks

Diagnosis: Minor scratches in the finish itself may look unsightly, but they are relatively easy to blend. Tiny cracks may simply be a symptom of crazing, or may in fact run deeper. A crack can indicate a serious structural problem, so look for the cause.

Remedy: Scratches and nicks can often be camouflaged with colored paste wax or removed by reamalgamation. If a scratch has cut all the way into the wood, though, it will have to be spot-stained to match the surrounding area before reamalgamation can begin. When wood is missing, repair the area by patching. Polyurethanes can't be reamalgamated; try overcoating after first roughing up the surface.

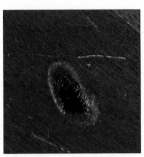

Scars, gouges, or burns

Diagnosis: These blemishes are often too conspicuous to be hidden by simple repairs. Either learn to live with them, or try to remove all the old finish and completely refinish the wood.

Remedy: If refinishing is out of the question, you might be able to repair a large defect by patching, either with shellac sticks or wax sticks. Before you patch a cigarette burn, be sure to scrape all the burned wood away from the area with a sharp knife or razor blade.

Crazing

Diagnosis: Crazing (or alligatoring, as it is sometimes called) is often caused by alternate expansion and contraction of wood under a finish. What you see is a dull, bumpy appearance or a pattern of very fine lines on a finished surface.

Remedy: If not too severe, this problem can be taken care of by abrasion or reamalgamation. Try sanding gently with fine (320- or 400-grit) sandpaper. If that doesn't work, determine the finish and rub with the appropriate solvent.

Worn or thin finishes

Diagnosis: Typical signs of a worn-out finish are scuff marks and dullness in areas of heaviest use, plus minute surface scratches and spots where the finish is worn completely through. Don't repair the surface too hastily: those signs of wear may be part of an old piece's charm.

Remedy: If damage is widespread, repair a worn or thin finish by lightly sanding, then padding or overcoating with a new finish. If necessary, touch up the original surface color first by staining worn areas with a dye stain to match the surrounding wood. If the worn area is small, a touch-up with a tinted oil finish may be all you need.

Dark spots or rings

Diagnosis: Dark, discolored spots are caused by water that has penetrated through the surface finish and into the wood. On a good finish, damage like this doesn't happen instantly but usually has a longer-range cause— for example, a flowerpot or something very moist that has been left on the wood for several days.

Remedy: The only way to get rid of dark spots and rings is to remove the entire finish. Once you reach bare wood, you can easily eliminate these marks with a solution of oxalic-acid crystals and water (see pages 42–43).

Can This Finish be Saved?

The hardest part of padding is finding the right materials. You'll need to purchase "padding lacquer," which is rarely sold in paint and hardware stores. You can obtain padding supplies from any large mail-order supplier (see page 14).

Prepare the padding cloth by rolling up a soft, clean piece of cotton (see drawing below) so it is large enough to fit comfortably in your hand. Dip the pad into a bowl of padding lacquer and squeeze it to remove any excess liquid.

Stroke the damaged wood surface with the moistened pad, using a small up-and-down rocking motion with your hand and wrist. This motion keeps the pad constantly moving at all times — an important consideration. Always start your padding motions gently, just wetting the surface. Increase pressure gradually to generate heat to help dry the lacquer.

Rub the wood with the pad for at least 15 minutes to make sure all the lacquer is dry. The completed finish will be quite glossy. If you want a dull shine instead, rub the surface with 4/0 steel wool or a finishing pad and apply a coat of paste wax.

THE PADDING MOTION

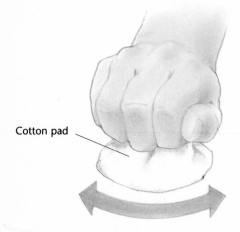

Cotton pad

SHELLAC-STICK PATCHING

A

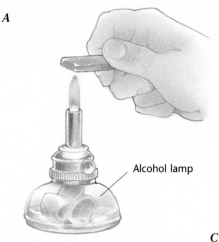

Alcohol lamp

B

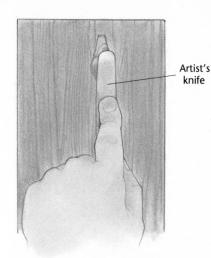

Artist's knife

C

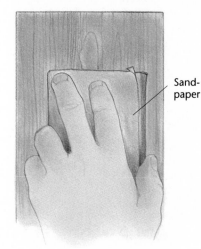

Sand-paper

To repair a large scratch *or gouge, melt shellac stick over heat source (A), press into wood (B), and smooth with fine sandpaper (C).*

Patching. Whenever you have a surface blemish in an otherwise fine furniture finish, try shellac-stick patching or wax-stick patching to camouflage the spot.

■ *Shellac-stick patching* is difficult to do without practice, so rehearse on a scrap of wood before you attempt to repair a valuable piece of furniture.

You may not be able to find quality shellac sticks in your area; in this case, you can order them by mail (see page 14). You'll also require an alcohol lamp, soldering iron, or refinisher's patching iron, as well as a flexible artist's knife (a grapefruit knife also works well).

Begin by choosing the shellac stick that most closely resembles the existing color of your wood. Heat the knife blade and the tip of the shellac stick over the heat source (see drawing above).

Apply the molten shellac to the damaged wood surface, using the hot knife to press the material smoothly into place. If the shellac cools too rapidly, reheat the knife blade and stroke over the hardened shellac again.

When the damaged area has been repaired and the shellac has cooled, shave off any excess shellac with a sharp razor blade. Carefully sand the repair with 400-grit water-proof sandpaper lubricated with paraffin oil. Finally, touch up the spot with a small artist's brush or by padding until it blends in with the surrounding surface.

■ *Wax-stick patching* is easier than shellac-stick patching, but less durable. Many wax-stick colors are blended especially for retouching furniture and are available at paint and hardware stores. Ordinary crayons can also do the job, if necessary.

If the repaired area is to receive significant wear, you'll want to prolong the life of the wax by covering it first with a coat of shellac and then with varnish or lacquer.

Stripping an Old Finish

If the methods described on pages 20–22 won't revive a finish to your satisfaction, or if you'd prefer a new stain or decorative treatment for your piece, the existing finish may require stripping.

Though it isn't difficult to remove an old finish, it's always a messy job. If you're not up to the task yourself, you can probably find a professional furniture refinisher who will do the stripping for you at a reasonable price. Be careful, though: commercial *dip-stripping* (in which the piece is immersed in a chemical bath) can loosen joints, damage veneers, or obscure the wood's color and figure.

Shopping for Strippers

Full-scale sanding may appear to be the quickest and easiest way to remove an old finish. But don't try it! Besides all the work involved, the trouble with sanding is that you can't remove the old finish without also removing some of the wood — and valuable surface patina.

In most cases, using a commercial paint and varnish remover is the most efficient way to take old furniture finishes down to bare wood. These removers contain a mixture of chemicals that work to soften an old finish so you can get it off by scraping gently with a putty knife or rubbing carefully with steel wool.

Traditionally, the best products have utilized methylene chloride. Many experienced refinishers feel that the higher the percentage of methylene chloride, the better. But methylene chloride is highly toxic, and new water-based products, kinder both to the user and to the environment, are appearing on the market. A possible drawback: water-based removers are slower-acting than methylene chloride, and the

longer soaking times some versions require can raise grain, buckle veneers, or even loosen joints if you're not careful.

Chemical removers are typically available in liquid, semipaste, and gel form. If you apply a large quantity of stripper to vertical surfaces, you'll appreciate the thicker consistency of a semipaste or gel. The less a remover drips, the longer it sticks to the surface, the more slowly it evaporates, and the more cutting power it provides in lifting the old finish from the bare wood. Liquid removers, on the other hand, seep into hard-to-reach corners and carvings; they're handy for a final "rinse" after the major stripping has been done.

The most expensive paint and varnish removers on the market are

A SAFE SETUP

Furniture finishing and refinishing should be easy, safe, and enjoyable. But before you undertake any project, keep these safety suggestions in mind:

■ When you're using finishing chemicals, work in a well-ventilated area (no closed garages or basements). Outdoors, of course, is safest. If you do work indoors, set up one or more portable fans and position them to circulate air and direct it out an open doorway or window.

■ Whenever possible, avoid breathing particles or vapors; a painter's mask and respirator, both shown on page 12, are smart investments if you plan to do much refinishing. Many finishing chemicals are caustic; don't let them contact your eyes or skin.

■ Keep all furniture-finishing materials away from children and animals. Read labels carefully — even some "environmentally safe" products are not completely nontoxic, or are so only when dry. Locked cabinets, especially if metal, are ideal for stor-

age. If an accident occurs, immediately call a physician.

■ Paint and varnish removers should not be stored for long periods of time. Excessive pressure may build up in an unopened can, causing the fluid to be sprayed on the user when the container is finally opened. Don't use stripper in direct sunlight.

■ Never apply finishing chemicals of any kind near an open flame, pilot light, electrical motor, or circuit that could produce open sparks. Needless to say, no smoking should be allowed in the work area. Spray-gun application of nitrocellulose-based lacquer is especially dangerous; don't spray this volatile product unless you have an approved spray booth. Always keep a recently charged fire extinguisher on hand just in case.

■ Rags and brushes soaked with furniture finishes are potential fire hazards and should be cleaned immediately or stored in a safe, well-ventilated place to prevent spontaneous combustion. Do not burn aerosol cans.

Stripping an Old Finish

"water-wash" blends. These contain waxes that mix freely with water and rinse away with a blast from the garden hose. Though these products are real time-savers, the water has a potentially damaging effect on any water-soluble glues used in the furniture's construction, and it will raise the grain of the wood. Water-wash removers can also destroy the attractive patina that lends value to some antiques.

The Stripping Process

Using a chemical remover correctly requires no great skill. The most important rule is to use it generously. But the removal of various kinds of finish is subject to different procedures, depending on the number of coats, the wood underneath, and the type of remover used. Be patient: it may take several passes to remove all the old layers.

Before you begin. The key to a painless stripping job is to be organized before you start.

It's a good idea to wear old clothes and to use sturdy rubber gloves and safety glasses. If the weather is agreeable, the best place to work is somewhere outdoors — but not in direct sunlight. Be sure to choose a nonflammable finish remover if you must work anywhere near an open flame, a pilot light, or a motor-driven electric appliance that might create sparks.

You'll want to put down paper or a large piece of cardboard to keep your work area clean. Don't depend on plastic painters' tarps, for many chemical removers can melt them. Elevate the legs of the piece of furniture on bricks or blocks; you could also set the legs inside buckets or coffee cans to handle some of the overflow.

Remove all knobs, handles, mirrors, and ornaments before you apply a chemical remover. Not only might they be damaged by contact with chemicals, but they are also much easier to clean and polish when not attached to the wood. If you need to strip hardware, put it — along with some stripper — in a sealed coffee can while you work on the main piece.

Dealing with upholstery has its own set of challenges. Removing old finish around the edges of upholstery is tedious, time-consuming, and risky. If the upholstery is in good shape and only the wood needs attention, play it safe by removing the fabric or having an upholsterer remove it for you.

Application tips. It's not hard to produce good results with any brand

STEP-BY-STEP STRIPPING

1 *Brush a thick coat of chemical stripper onto wood, working it into all nooks and crannies. Don't "worry" the surface with extra brush strokes; instead, let the stripper do the work.*

2 *Let the piece sit for the recommended time — this water-based remover takes 30 minutes. Then slide off loosened finish in line with wood grain, using plastic scraper or putty knife. If stripper is working effectively, you won't need to scrape.*

of remover if you follow these basic steps:

■ First, pour the remover into an unbreakable plastic pail. Spread it on as thickly as possible, using an old paintbrush with a wooden handle and natural bristles. (Removers can melt synthetic bristles.) Avoid brushing back and forth once the remover is on the surface: such brushing causes faster evaporation and prevents the chemicals from doing their job. If the surface looks dull or if there doesn't seem to be enough remover in certain spots, only then should you brush on more.

■ After the appropriate wait (5 to 15 minutes for methylene chloride, 30 minutes or longer for water-based stripper), check to see that the thick coating has done its work. Many strippers give varnish or paint a wrinkled look when their action is accomplished; not all water-based products have this effect.

■ Take a flexible putty knife and gently slide the old finish off all flat surfaces, working in the direction of the grain and guiding the mess into a cardboard box or metal bucket. Use coarse steel wool or a coarse synthetic finishing pad to strip contoured surfaces.

■ For cleaning out small areas around carvings, moldings, corners, or details of any kind, try using cotton swabs, an old toothbrush, or even a soft brass-bristle brush. Or sprinkle clean wood shavings on the area and brush them away after they've soaked up the residue.

■ Some refinishers switch from semipaste or gel to liquid remover for a final wash after most of the finish has been removed. Whether you do this or not, use paper towels or rags, as a final step, to wipe the surface clean.

■ Stripper may not reach traces of paint, stain, or dark spots that have lodged in the wood pores. A brisk rubbing with a brass-bristle brush should remove paint; stubborn stains may require oxalic acid or chlorine bleach (see pages 42–43).

Cleaning up. Wait for the stripped piece to dry slightly before you inspect it. You'll find that even the most careful application of a chemical remover will leave some remnants of the old finish on the surface or in the grain. And if you've used an inexpensive remover, you might even find a film of wax coating the wood. Such residues must be cleaned off, or they will interfere with staining and final finishing.

For large areas, use 1/0 or 2/0 steel wool or a finishing pad with paint thinner or denatured alcohol for cleanup. Work on small areas with cotton swabs or a toothbrush. To complete the job, buff the piece with a solvent-dampened cloth.

3 *A brass-bristle brush removes finish from hard-to-reach seams, corners, and carvings; cotton swabs or a toothbrush can also do the job. Use paper towels or rags to wipe up excess gunk.*

4 *Clean up stripped surfaces as required, rubbing with steel wool or finishing pad and paint thinner or alcohol. To finish up, buff piece with solvent-dampened cloth.*

Don't "over-repair" an old favorite — those dents and dings are often part of the soul of the piece. These antiques sport scratches, worm holes, and cracks aplenty; such marks are simply highlighted and protected with hand-rubbed beeswax.

Basic Furniture Repairs

As soon as the old finish has been totally removed, analyze the wood surface to make sure that it's ready for smoothing. You may find that some repairs are needed, especially on very old pieces. Begin by looking for the most common signs of distress: loose drawers, broken or missing chair pieces, cracked tabletops, or fractured legs. Also check for deep gouges, dents, or blemishes that could detract from the final refinished effect.

Most furniture repairs are not difficult to make if you have patience and a few basic tools. If, however, a technique seems beyond you, or if you're dealing with a valuable antique, don't hesitate to throw in the towel and consult a professional. Whatever your piece's vintage, resist the impulse to make quick repairs using nails, screws, or mending plates. Sooner or later, such fasteners cause more problems than they solve.

To simplify furniture repairs, divide whatever work needs to be done into three classifications: regluing, replacing parts, and repairing the surface.

■ *Disassemble and reglue* any joints, drawers, spindles, backs, arms, and legs that have loosened. Glue and clamp any cracks in the wood.

■ *Replace* any missing wooden parts—shattered tabletops, unrepairable chair legs and arms, decorative moldings, leg supports, feet, or wooden knobs. Be sure such replacements have been made before you approach the final wood smoothing.

■ *Repair* gouges, dents, veneer blemishes, and all minor imperfections. Some of these small repairs may have to be made after the first coat of stain is applied to ensure that the color of the repair matches the color of the stained wood.

Repairing Loose Joints

Loose joints and cracks should be the first things you fix. When a joint is loose, movement is caused in other furniture parts, resulting in still more damage. One loose joint, if not corrected, can eventually cause the entire piece of furniture to fall apart.

Basic anatomy. Before attacking a wobbly chair or table, it helps to have a general understanding of furniture components and joinery.

Despite the diversity of types and styles, most fine furniture has the same basic structure (called leg-and-rail or frame construction) and shares many of the same parts.

To illustrate this point, consider a bed: four vertical members, referred to as *legs* or *posts,* are connected to four horizontal pieces, called *rails,* to form the frame. Reduce the dimensions of the bed, add height to the legs, secure a top to the rails, and you have a table or desk. Reduce the dimensions even more, shorten the legs, add lower rails (called *stretchers)* and a back, and the structure becomes a rudimentary chair.

For connecting these members, some type of mortise-and-tenon joint (see drawing above right) is traditional. Alternatively, look for a

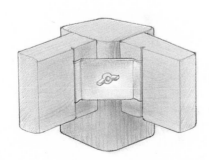
Leg-mounting plate

FURNITURE JOINTS

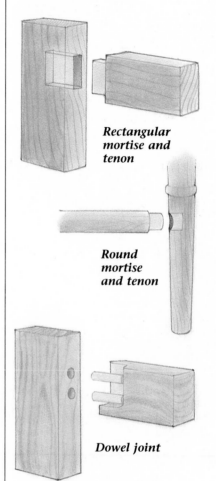

Rectangular mortise and tenon

Round mortise and tenon

Dowel joint

Housed joint

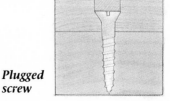
Plugged screw

Basic Furniture Repairs

simple *butt* joint reinforced with two *blind dowels*.

Though chair arms can be joined to back posts with a butt joint reinforced with a screw, traditional joinery calls for *housing* the arm — cutting a recess in the post to receive it. The front post is usually tenoned into the arm.

You may also come across screws, through dowels or plugged screws, knock-down hardware, or hidden splines. Watch for finishing nails or mending plates used in past repairs, and plan to remove these.

Choosing the right glue. Effective gluing is central to the stability of most joints, and to the success of your repair. If your problem is simple, such as a loose chair spindle or leg, it's handy to use ordinary white glue, which needs no mixing and is easy to apply. Or you may prefer a yellow (aliphatic resin) glue, which is similar to white glue but has a slightly shorter drying time and gives a slightly stronger hold.

Modern adhesives have largely supplanted the hot animal-hide glue used in most furniture until the 1940s. But because of its extended open (working) time and its ability to bond to itself (even new to old), hide glue is still unsurpassed. It can be purchased in flake or pearl form from mail-order sources (see page 14); before use, it must be mixed with water and heated. A slightly weaker cousin, liquid hide glue, is more convenient to use.

Plastic resin, resorcinol, and epoxy glues are sometimes used to mend a spot that must undergo much stress, such as a cracked chair leg. But because the resulting bond is irreversible, you'll want to use such glues only when their great strength is required.

BREAKING DOWN A JOINT

To disassemble furniture joints, rap gently with a rubber- or rawhide-faced mallet.

Breaking it down. Disassemble your furniture as required before making repairs. Carefully remove all screws and knock glued sections apart with a rubber- or rawhide-faced mallet. Joints fastened with animal-hide glue can be loosened with a little alcohol; you can reach stubborn spots with a hypodermic-like glue injector (available at hardware and craft stores). Hot water and vinegar may loosen white or yellow glues. Try acetone or lacquer thinner on other glues (but be careful: these substances can dissolve an existing finish).

You may encounter buried nails used in past repairs. If so, carefully dig out the heads, then pull them with a pair of pliers or a cat's claw. Follow an orderly sequence as you work, noting how assemblies and subassemblies fit together.

Any old glue that remains in a joint may inhibit the bonding of the new glue, so you should lightly clean away all old glue from the individual pieces. Hide glue is easy to remove with water. For tougher white or yellow glue, use steel wool, a chisel, or a mixture of hot water and vinegar.

If an old joint is loose but you can't get it completely apart without damage to the surrounding wood, squirt a little hide glue behind the joint where it will do the most good. This method is frequently used with white or yellow glue. But these glues won't stick to old, dirty glue and wood.

Even gluing can't do the job if the joint isn't a good press-fit to begin with. It may be necessary to shape and glue extra wood to one or more parts (see drawing on facing page) of the joint. Build up spindles (round tenons) with wood shavings or wrapped string; on rectangular mortise-and-tenon joints, shimming works well. Broken dowels may be removed with a slightly undersize drill bit; clean the hole with a bit that's the correct size, then replace the dowel.

Clamping it up. Never glue without clamping, since all newly glued joints require some form of pressure while they are drying to achieve the best possible bond. Hardware stores carry several kinds of woodworking clamps that are handy to use. Bar and pipe clamps are best for bridging long distances; C-clamps and spring clamps are good for small jobs. These items are often expensive, though, and the creative home refinisher may find that many common household objects work just as well.

Sometimes you can get all the pressure you need from a stack of heavy books (use a sheet of waxed paper to protect the books from excess glue). Or you might try a few loops of clothesline or cut-up inner tubes, wrapped around the furniture and twisted tight with a stick. With a little imagination, you can devise any number of pressure-producing devices, depending on the particular clamping problem at hand.

Contoured clamping blocks like the ones shown on page 30 help keep even pressure on irregularly shaped parts; cut them from ¾-inch plywood or solid stock. Clamp jaws may mar wood surfaces, so line them with scrap blocks, waxed paper, or plastic clamp pads (which make gluing up a lot easier).

Before tightening clamps fully, check the assembly's alignment. Now's the time for any adjustments: loosen the clamps slightly; realign any offending pieces; retighten; and recheck. A partner can help position long clamps.

When everything's perfectly aligned, tighten the clamps until they're snug but not too tight; if you see a thin bead of glue along the joint, it means you have the right pressure.

Once a dowel joint or mortise-and-tenon joint is pulled tight, you may be able to remove the clamp and use it elsewhere.

Wobbly table hardware. Many tables have legs fastened to the stretcher or apron with bolts — sometimes directly, sometimes through a leg-mounting block or plate (see drawing on page 27). Sometimes a wobbly leg can be corrected by simply tightening a bolt. But if you leave

CLAMPING UP

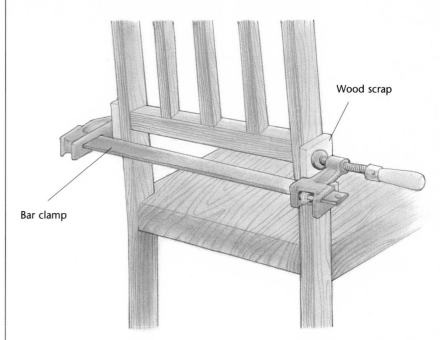

Wood scrap

Bar clamp

Reassemble repaired joints *as required, lining clamp jaws with wood scraps. Have a helper on hand for large or awkward jobs.*

such a problem unattended, the next stage can be a crack or break in the leg-mounting block or in the table leg itself.

A wooden leg-mounting block is usually an easy repair if you have

basic woodworking tools. Just copy the old block, redrill the bolt hole, and reattach. If the bolt has broken out of the leg, use the repair method described on page 31 to fill the hole.

REPAIRING A JOINT

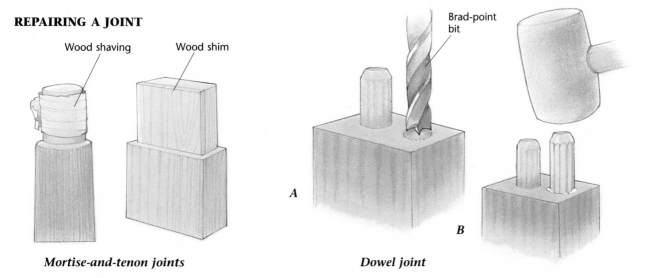

Wood shaving   Wood shim

Brad-point bit

A

B

Mortise-and-tenon joints   **Dowel joint**

Rebuild damaged joints *before assembly. Loose mortise-and-tenon joints (left) are easy to fix; thicken them with wood shavings or shims. Broken dowel joints (right) are trickier: drill out old dowel (A), then tap new glue-covered dowel into place (B).*

Basic Furniture Repairs

Repairing Deep Cracks & Breaks

Repair cracks in tabletops, drawers, and chair seats before they crack any further. Shallow cracks or crazing can often be fixed cosmetically, but don't surface-treat deep cracks. The underlying problem won't go away.

When cracks are simple, with-the-grain fractures, the pieces will usually fit back together quite well, and gluing and clamping may be all that is needed. If the two sections on either side of the crack have not totally separated, it may be possible to work glue down into the opening by rocking the two sections back and forth with your hands; a glue injector is another possibility. (But remember: white and yellow glues can't work unless the mating surfaces are clean — use sandpaper on edge.) Apply one or more clamps to keep the crack closed while the glue is drying. Wash or wipe off all excess glue.

Cross-grain cracks and breaks are tougher to remedy. If you feel that gluing alone won't supply a strong enough bond to support the weight of a particular furniture piece, insert a dowel (see page 29) into both sides of the cracked area for additional stability.

Sometimes wood fibers are so completely torn that the pieces will not easily fit together again. In this case, cut the cracked portion entirely away (see drawing on facing page), fit a new insert in its place, and glue. When your newly repaired section is dry, camouflage it to match the rest of the piece.

Replacing Missing Wood

If a piece of wood is too badly broken to be repaired, or if a fragment is missing entirely, replacement is the only solution. You must decide whether your furniture piece is really worth all the time you will have to spend restoring it to its original condition. If only one or two minor pieces of wood are missing and if the style of the piece particularly appeals to you, go ahead and try your hand at reconstruction. Major restorations, though, are usually best left to the experts.

To start, you'll need to find the right kind of wood to match your piece. Many types and figures of wood are hard to find today, and it can be difficult, even when you do get the kind you require, to match a newly sawn piece to an older piece of the same species. Secondhand stores, thrift shops, junkyards, and garage sales are good places to look for leaves from mahogany, cherry, walnut, oak, and other wooden tables. Collecting furniture "wrecks" keeps many a restorer in fine aged wood.

FIXING A DEEP CRACK

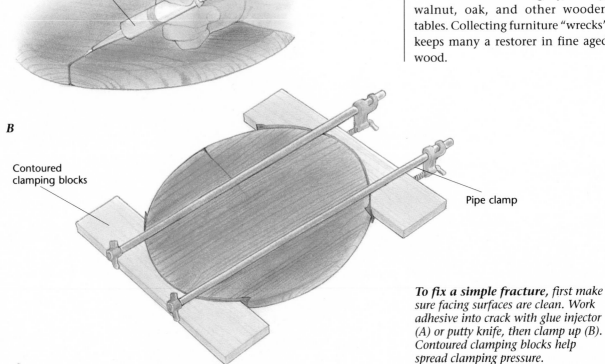

A Glue injector

B Contoured clamping blocks

Pipe clamp

To fix a simple fracture, first make sure facing surfaces are clean. Work adhesive into crack with glue injector (A) or putty knife, then clamp up (B). Contoured clamping blocks help spread clamping pressure.

REPLACING DAMAGED WOOD

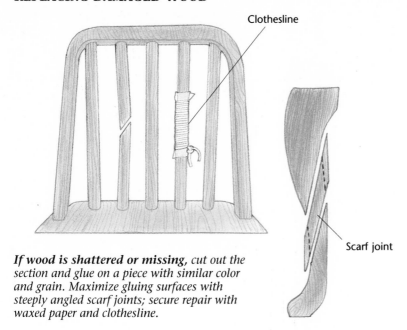

Clothesline

Scarf joint

If wood is shattered or missing, cut out the section and glue on a piece with similar color and grain. Maximize gluing surfaces with steeply angled scarf joints; secure repair with waxed paper and clothesline.

Rectangular and round profiles are relatively easy to copy; other shapes may require lathing, bending, or other shaping to mimic the original form. Try to replace the minimum amount necessary to make the repair. Join the new piece to existing wood with a long, tapered scarf joint to provide the maximum gluing surface.

Fitting a new section into existing furniture can require some ingenuity. For instance, how do you replace a spindle that fits into a socket at both ends, unless you disassemble the furniture? Solve this particular problem by cutting the new part into two pieces with a tapered splice across the center. After fitting a piece into the socket at each end, simply glue and clamp the splice together.

Loose Screws & Hinges

It's not just wood that tires out over the years: hardware wears out, too. Door hinges, table-leaf hinges, and stripped screws are all, fortunately, easy to adjust.

Door woes. Often, simply tightening loose hinges gets a sagging door back in alignment. First, clean off any dirt and straighten any bent hinges in a vise. Tighten any loose hinge screws. If they can't be tightened, repair the screw holes as shown below right and replace the screws.

If the door binds badly or isn't square in its frame, the hinges may have to be shimmed or set in deeper mortises. Deepen the mortises as a last resort; achieving just the right depth can be tricky. If you must remove excess wood from the edges of a binding door, sand with coarse and then finer sandpaper.

If the door is warped, you may be able to "unbend" it; see page 34 for more information.

Loose table-leaf hinges. Loose table leaves lead to bent hinges, bent screws, and torn wood if ignored for very long. If you have these troubles, first try tightening the screws. If they won't tighten, you'll need to fill in the stripped-out holes with wood dough or plastic wood, toothpicks, or matchsticks; redrill the holes; and try the screws again. If a hinge is bent, straighten it carefully in a vise. Subtle changes in leaf height can be accomplished by alternately shimming below one hinge or deepening the mortise on the other.

Stripped fasteners. Rusty or abused screws can make any do-it-yourselfer's day a nightmare. If the screw is merely frozen, apply lubricating oil first. Otherwise, drill out the center; or dig it out however possible and use locking pliers to rotate it the rest of the way.

SCREW & HINGE REPAIRS

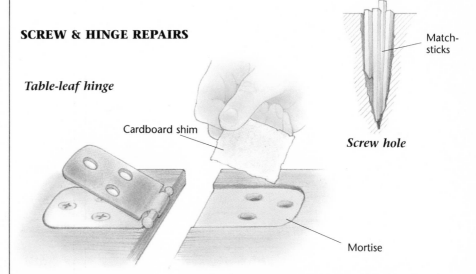

Table-leaf hinge

Cardboard shim

Match-sticks

Screw hole

Mortise

Hardware woes require some sleight-of-hand repairs. Pack stripped or oversize screw holes (top right) with matchsticks or dowels; add new screw. Change leaf hinge alignment (bottom left) by raising with shims or deepening mortise.

Basic Furniture Repairs

Drawer Defects

Drawers get such heavy use that they frequently develop irritating ailments. Most of the troubles are caused by overworn surfaces that make a drawer slide crookedly until it binds and sticks. Other times, a drawer bottom comes loose, racking the frame out of square. And in other cases, the basic box simply needs regluing.

Before resorting to carpentry on a balky drawer, try applying a lubricating coat of paraffin on the sliding surfaces. Also hunt for small stray objects in the drawer's space. A single lost safety pin can cause remarkable resistance to orderly operation.

Drawers that do not close fully. Typically, side rails or guides provide the surfaces on which a drawer slides; extra-wide drawers may have an added guide centered under the bottom. When a drawer does not close properly, the cause is usually uneven wear on the sliding surfaces.

If a drawer appears to be canted in the space, one rail probably has worn down or split off. The cure is a new rail.

If a drawer slides most of the way closed, but stops an inch short, both rails have worn down so that the face of the drawer catches on the front of the cabinet. (In such a case, the drawer will close if it is lifted up and then pushed the last inch.)

Drawers that stick. A drawer that has swollen tight against its opening can usually be cured by sanding, once you determine where the tight spot is. Remove the problem drawer and look for any unusually burnished wood.

If guides appear to be in good condition and the drawer will slide part way in or out freely before it sticks, either the drawer or the cabinet may be out of square. A loose or crooked drawer should be taken apart and reglued (see below). If the cabinet itself is to blame, adjusting the guides may be the only remedy. Check guide alignment with a carpenter's square, then either replace the part with a new one or shim the existing strip to the correct width.

A drawer that fits so loosely it strays off course needs its guides adjusted to fit more tightly.

Drawer reconstruction. A drawer is simply a box within a box, and sometimes the pieces can't hold up to the constant slamming they take. Broken or warped bottoms are quite common, and easy to replace. Cut a new bottom from hardwood plywood, particle board, or solid lumber to match the existing material

DRAWER ANATOMY

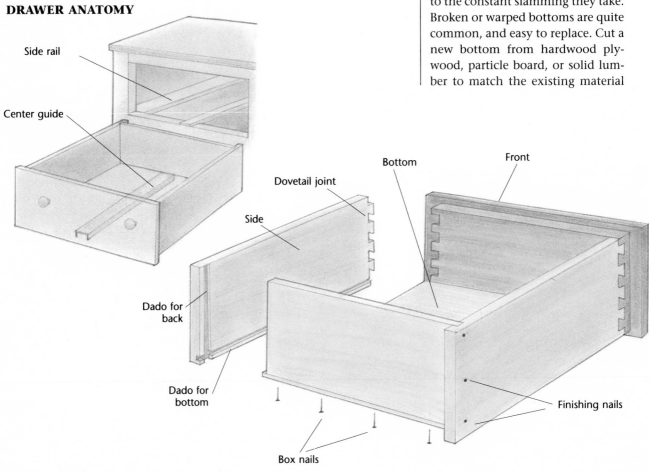

Side rail

Center guide

Dado for back

Dado for bottom

Box nails

Dovetail joint

Side

Bottom

Front

Finishing nails

(most drawers have ¼-inch-thick bottoms). Don't glue the bottom into the dadoes (you need to allow for seasonal wood movement); instead, simply tack it to the back piece.

If the bottom is loose, it's probably due to a split in the side piece below the dado that houses the bottom. Simply cut the existing side piece off square, add a new strip, and refashion the dado if required.

If the front, back, or sides are loose, remove the bottom, gently knock the pieces apart, clean the areas, and reglue. Be careful of dovetail joints: they're easy to split. If the original adhesive was hide glue, you're in luck: it's easy to melt and clean (see page 28). If not, remove the old glue as best you can.

Reassemble the drawer frame piece by piece, then slide in the bottom. The bottom usually squares the frame; if not, clamp it square. Check what's square by measuring the diagonals; if the drawer is square, these measurements will match.

Veneer Repairs

Veneers — thin strips of fine furniture wood glued onto a more pedestrian core — have been used to dress up furniture for hundreds of years. But they begin, inevitably, to loosen or chip. Before abandoning the piece to the basement or sending it to a refinisher's shop, you may want to try some basic repairs.

Regluing loose veneer. At some point, veneer begins to peel away from the core. Check any furniture piece — especially one you've just stripped — by tapping with your fingertip across the surface and listening for a hollow, thumping sound.

If your piece was built before the 1940s and hasn't been repaired since, its veneers are almost certainly held down by animal-hide glue. You can take advantage of hide glue's ability to reverse itself by melting it, using a clothes iron set on LOW to apply heat over a damp cloth (see

REPLACING VENEER

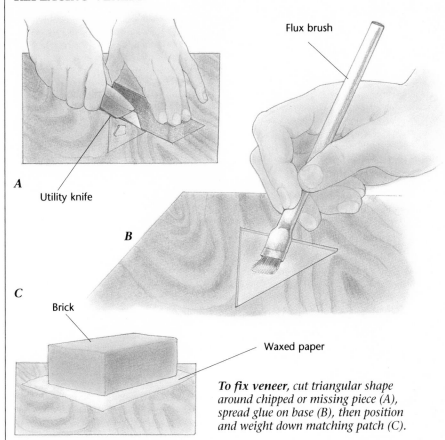

To fix veneer, cut triangular shape around chipped or missing piece (A), spread glue on base (B), then position and weight down matching patch (C).

drawing on page 34). Press the veneer into place; if it seems loose, add waxed paper on top and clamp or weight it overnight.

If a veneer has blistered, carefully slice an X through the area with a sharp utility knife. If you're using hide glue, just smooth things out below; but if you're using white or yellow glue, the base must be really clean in order for the new glue to adhere. Contact cement is often used for veneer repairs, but will present real problems in any future repairs.

Loose veneer along an edge is simpler to deal with. Work sandpaper under the edge to clean, then shoot glue in with a glue injector. Clamp or weight the area overnight.

Repairing chipped or damaged veneer. Veneer along the edge of a tabletop, desk, or drawer front may

be chipped or missing altogether. If you have the chip, by all means save it; if the break is clean, it's easy to reglue. If a section of veneer is badly damaged or missing, you'll need to cut a new piece and patch it in. If done with care, the patch will blend in, once refinished.

The trick is to find new veneer that matches the wood species, thickness, and grain of the original veneer. Veneer specialty shops and mail-order firms are two places to look; and garage sales and junk shops may turn up worn but salvageable veneered furniture. If all else fails, you might take an existing piece from a concealed area and make the visible patch, replacing it with new veneer in the hidden area.

Either match the missing piece exactly with a tracing (tough to do) or cut a larger triangle (as shown above) in line with the grain. Shape

Basic Furniture Repairs

the new piece, matching the grain direction as closely as possible. Clean the wooden base, then dry-fit the veneer patch. Make small adjustments with a plane or file. Spread glue on the base only, position the veneer patch, lay down waxed paper, and clamp or weight the area. Once the glue is dry, you can stain and/or finish the new section of veneer to match the rest of the surface.

Curved surfaces are tougher to fix. One suggestion is to use a combination of heat (a clothes iron set on LOW) and moisture to gently bend the veneer to shape it. These can be rough assignments, and like replacing large sections of old veneer, may call for an expert's touch.

Coping with Warped Boards

Warps result when wood fibers on one side of a board contain more moisture than those on the other side. The problem often arises when one side of the wood is unfinished.

Before replacing warped wood, try to repair it by drying out the convex side or by adding more moisture to the concave side. You can do this easily by placing the warped piece, concave side down, on a moist surface under a heat lamp or other heat source for a few days. Even the most curved of boards may straighten out again. Seal any unfinished surfaces with a coat of shellac or varnish to ward off future problems.

Kerfing with a power saw — making numerous parallel cuts partway through the wood — is sometimes recommended for the underside of a warped tabletop; after straightening, the piece can be splinted across the kerfs. But this procedure won't necessarily prevent warping in the future. And do you really want to intervene so drastically in the case of a valued heirloom?

Dents, Nicks & Gouges

Much old furniture is structurally sound, with only a few scrapes, scratches, or nicks to reveal the amount of use it has received. Even a new piece of unfinished furniture may have marks to show for the time it spent on a dealer's display floor. A certain "distressed" look is evident on all pieces of wood, regardless of origin or age, and is something that can't be helped. Indeed, the value of many antiques is enhanced by subtle wear marks that prove authenticity.

Very little can or should be done to cover up such signs of actual wear, but it's best to repair scratches, nicked corners, and surface dents before a new finish is applied. Here's how.

Fixing dents. Dents are found on nearly every piece of well-used furniture. If the bruise is shallow, you may be able to return the compressed wood fibers to their original condition by wetting them with water to make them swell. For proper moisture penetration, be sure that all finish is removed from around the surface of the dent — or puncture the existing finish with tiny pinholes.

When water alone won't raise a dent, place a damp cloth and the tip of a clothes iron (set on LOW) over the dent for a few seconds and again watch for the wood fibers to swell. You may have to do this several times, applying heat for a few seconds at a time. When the grain in the dent has been raised to the level of the surrounding surface, remove the iron and cloth and prepare the rest of the surface for sanding.

If the dent still hangs tough, you can always resort to patching (see below).

Scars and nicks. These blemishes always result in the loss of some wood. Fill them with one of three standbys: wood dough, wood putty, or plastic wood.

Using patching materials to make surface repairs presents a problem if you're planning to apply a clear finish: patching materials have a different rate of absorption than the surrounding wood, and patched areas tend to look lighter or darker than the rest of the piece once stain

STEAMING OUT A DENT

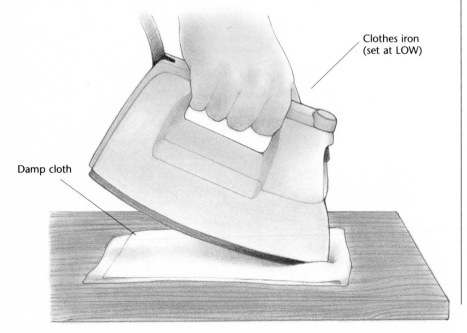

Clothes iron (set at LOW)

Damp cloth

or a clear finish is applied. An effective (though time-consuming) solution is to test your patching material, stain, and top coat on a piece of scrap wood or an out-of-the-way part of your piece. You can then adjust the color of the patching material more precisely.

Wood dough comes in a range of shades and tends to soak up a good deal of stain. Wood putty is whitish gray in color and comes premixed or in powder form; choose premixed for small imperfections, powder (to mix with water) for large voids. Though some putties will accept stain, they're most useful under opaque finishes. Plastic wood, which comes in a wide variety of wood tones, will absorb very little stain.

You can apply any of these compounds with a putty knife. On large voids, use two or three thin applications, leaving the last layer a little higher than the surface of the wood (you'll sand it down later).

Shellac sticks (see page 22) also work well for small checks, dings, and scratches; choose the color closest to your final finish.

Gouges. These defects often go considerably deeper than simple scars and nicks. In some cases, you will have to use small pieces of wood to replace areas that are too large to be corrected by any other method.

When repairing the damaged corner of a table, your success depends on how well you match the type and grain direction of the new wood to the existing stock. Cut out both the defect and the replacement at the same angle, and glue the new piece in place. When the repair has dried, use a file or electric router to shape it to match the surrounding wood.

To fix smaller gashes, such as those that often occur on the edges of table legs, glue a new piece of wood into the indentation and let the area dry thoroughly; then file or plane away any excess wood.

PATCHING

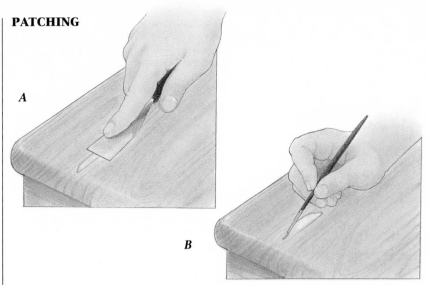

Fill surface blemishes with patching material and a putty knife (A), sanding when dry; build up additional layers as required. Use an artist's brush (B) to touch up color.

SHAPING A NEW CORNER

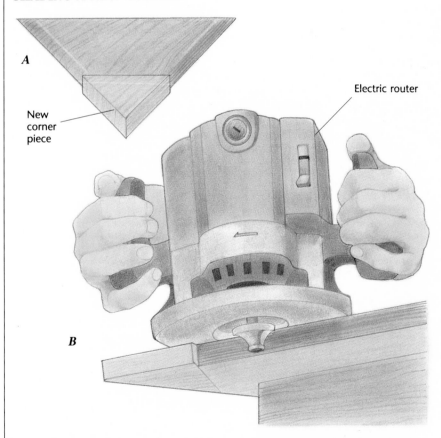

If a corner is badly gouged, consider replacing it. Cut off damaged wood cleanly, then glue on new piece (A). An electric router (B) can reproduce some edge profiles; otherwise, shape replacement with hand tools.

Preparing the Surface

Whether your furniture piece needs finishing or refinishing, surface preparation is crucial to the quality of its final look. It also requires patient attention to detail. But take a tip from the pros, and spend that extra effort on smoothing, bleaching, and sealing. You'll be glad you did.

If you're refinishing, you'll first take the old finish down to bare wood, then smooth away any residual trace of the old finish and prepare the surface as if the wood were new. A new woodworking project will require spot repairs, glue scraping, and careful sanding. Even unfinished furniture pieces need some detail work before you apply the finish of your choice.

Smoothing — with sandpaper, steel wool, or a finishing pad — is the most important operation in preparing a wood surface for a finish. Bleaching is helpful in certain cases: bleach can remove dark spots or lingering traces of an old stain and can lighten or even out the color of darker woods before restaining and/or finishing. Tired of clean white boards and plywoods blotching when stain is applied? A sealer brushed on before staining softwoods will help smooth the color. See page 43 for details.

Final smoothing — using sandpaper, steel wool, or a finishing pad — is a must for almost all furniture projects, including freshly stripped pieces. A finishing sander makes short work of smoothing this walnut surface. Always finish-sand directly in line with wood grain.

Smoothing the Wood

Though you may have spent hours staining, finishing, and polishing, if the surface of your piece has any traces of roughness, the final finish will only emphasize these shortcomings. By investing some time with sandpaper, steel wool, or finishing pad, you can make traces of old stain, tool marks, water marks, and other irregularities disappear, so the finish will enhance the intrinsic beauty of the wood.

Sandpaper or Steel Wool?

Sandpaper can be a boon to the home woodworker, but it's a tool that seems to inspire overuse. Its rapidly abrasive action has potential to harm as well as help. In seconds, the heavy hand of a careless refinisher using sandpaper can destroy the distinctive tool marks and beautiful patina on a fine antique.

For those situations where too much sanding could be harmful (on veneers, for example), steel wool or a finishing pad is a better choice. Some professional refinishers use nothing else.

Choosing sandpaper.
Sandpaper is sandpaper, right? Actually, it's not even made with sand. The material and type you use depend on the results you want to achieve.

Flint paper, beige in color, is the least expensive but also the least durable and least effective option.

Garnet paper, which is reddish to golden brown, provides excellent results for hand sanding, especially in the final stages.

Aluminum oxide paper (sometimes labeled *production* paper), light gray to grayish brown, is a synthetic material of great toughness; choose it for rough-to-medium hand sanding or for use with a power sander's belt or pad.

Silicon carbide paper, blue-gray to charcoal, is often called *wet-or-dry* because its waterproof backing allows you to use it wet, thus eliminating the clogging tendency of its tiny grains. You can use it to give wood a final polish or to cut excess gloss between finish coats.

The sandpaper's type is usually identified on the back side of each sheet. Other information you'll find there includes grit number, backing weight, and the distinction of open or closed coat.

Grit numbers run from 12 to 600, but 50 (very coarse) to 240 (very fine) is the common range. Wet-or-dry paper is generally available up to 600 grit.

Backing weight is rated from A (thinnest) to E. In general, backing weight decreases as grit becomes finer.

Closed-coat sandpaper has more particles, so it can cut faster; but it tends to clog on softwoods or old finishes. Open-coat sandpaper works better for rough sanding.

Steel wool.
Purchased in the form of pads and available in several grades, steel wool is popular for smoothing off newly stripped wood surfaces and for light buffing between finish coats.

Grade 1/0 is used chiefly for general cleaning and smoothing — particularly after finish removers have done their job. Grades 2/0 and 3/0 are fine-textured and often used for smoothing a surface before the finish goes on. Grade 4/0 has a very fine texture and is perfect for smoothing between final finishing coats.

Finishing pads.
These thin woven sheets, reminiscent of kitchen scrub pads, are a modern version of steel wool. They vary in both coarseness and size. Unlike steel wool, these pads won't shed or rust; also, they can be cleaned with water and reused.

Mechanical or Hand Sanding?

Sanding can be done by hand or by machine. A power sander undoubtedly provides the fastest sanding, but you should practice handling one before you try using it for fine furniture work. Sanding by hand is slower but safer, permitting you to be more sensitive in treating surface irregularities. Hand sanding with a sanding block often results in a smoother final product.

Power sanders consist of three main types: finishing sanders, belt sanders, and disc sanders.

■ *Finishing sanders* work at very high speeds to produce a fine, controlled finish; they won't remove much stock, even when filled with coarse sandpaper.

Though most finishing sanders have either straight-line or orbital action, some allow you to switch from one motion to the other. Straight-line action theoretically produces a finer finish, since the stroke is always in line with the grain; but because an orbital sander moves in tight circles — up to 12,000 orbits per minute — it gives a fine polishing effect.

Finishing sanders range in pad size from 4 by 4⅜ inches to about 4½ by 9⅝ inches. The smaller sizes, designed to be held in one hand, allow you to sand vertical and overhead surfaces comfortably.

■ *Belt sanders* are the fastest straight-line sanders around; the abrasive moves constantly against the wood, on a continually revolving belt. Though a belt sander is more diffi-

Sanding blocks

Belt sander

Hand scrapers

Finishing sander

KUNZ

SANDVIK

Finishing pad

Steel wool

Drum sanders

Wet-or-dry sandpaper

Garnet sandpaper

Production paper

PORTER·C

Smoothing the Wood

cult to use than a finishing sander, it can rough-sand large quantities of flat material or even strip off old finishes from tabletops without the application of chemical remover.

Belt sanders are labeled by the width and length of the belt. The most popular sizes are 3 by 21, 3 by 24, and 4 by 24 inches. The relatively small, light, 3- by 21-inch model is the best choice for most woodworking tasks. Be very careful, though: any belt sander can remove a lot of material quickly.

■ *Disc sanders* are not recommended for delicate sanding of furniture. Both the large commercial kind and the small ones that can be attached to a power drill are hard to handle, and they remove too much material too quickly. In addition, disc sanders leave large cross-grain marks that are difficult to remove. Fitted with a buffing pad, though, these machines can be very useful for buffing wax to a high gloss (see page 75).

Hand sanding. Even though rapid power sanding does a good job in most cases, many wood-finishing experts recommend that the very last sanding be done by hand.

For successful hand sanding, it's best to support the sandpaper with something in addition to your fingers. A sanding block, available at paint and hardware stores in various sizes and styles, gives good support. Or you can make your own device: just wrap the abrasive around a wooden block faced with a ½-inch-thick sheet of sponge rubber or felt.

Surface Sanding Techniques

Begin by examining the piece to be smoothed in a good light to locate any major defects on the surface. If you discover dents, gouges, nicks, or cracks that need to be corrected, see Chapter 2, "Stripping & Repairs." Then proceed to sanding — doing only as much as is necessary to clean and smooth the surface. Stripped or patched surfaces may require rough sanding. But a clean, new piece may

need only a light pass with very fine sandpaper.

Rough sanding. If the previous finish of your furniture has just been removed or if the wood surface is otherwise in bad shape, choose a fairly coarse abrasive (120 to 150 grit) and cautiously sand the surface, working in the direction of the wood's grain. This will level ridges and remove any chemical residue, glue stains, or other discolorations, but it will also leave small scratches over the entire surface of your piece.

Follow this initial sanding with a medium-grit abrasive (180 to 220 grit). Take your time, and work carefully; any cross-grain scratches made at this point will be magnified by a clear finish. On end grain, move straight across in one direction only, so you don't round the edges. Continue this second step until all the small scratches produced by the first sanding have been removed.

Between sandings, wipe the piece carefully with a rag moistened

CONTOUR SANDING

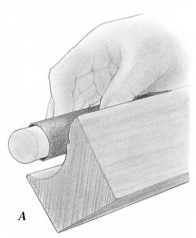

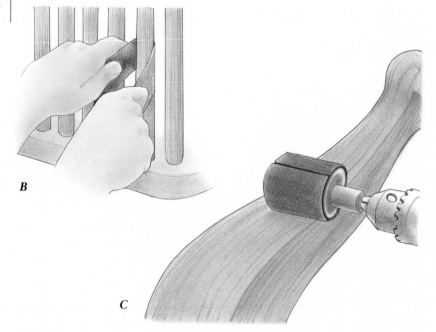

Curved surfaces can call for special tricks — such as a contoured wood scrap to serve as a sanding block (A), a sandpaper strip used "shoeshine-style" (B), and a drum sander accessory fitted to an electric drill (C).

with paint thinner — a few stray grits can ruin the fine surface you're trying to achieve.

Finish sanding. To complete the job, change to a fine grade of abrasive paper (240 to 320 grit) and sand directly with the grain, using long, even strokes. To check for smoothness, place a light behind the surface and bend down to observe the light's reflection. Go over any irregularities you might find, and then check once more.

Raising the grain. When wood is exposed to moisture, the fibers begin to swell, making the surface look and feel fuzzy. Some woodworkers wet the wood before finishing so they can sand down these fibers.

Is it helpful to raise the grain? Definitely, if you're using a water-based stain or finish. But with other treatments, you won't need to raise the grain unless the piece is to have a penetrating finish and be placed in a moist environment.

Sanding curves. Contour sanding is tough because there's no flat surface for the sanding block or power sander's belt or pad. Hand-sanding tricks include folding up an older, broken-down sandpaper sheet to follow the curves, wrapping the paper around a dowel or contoured scrap, and using a thin strip "shoeshine-style" (see drawing on facing page).

To work on a curve with a large radius, try replacing the felt pad on the bottom of your finishing sander with a rubber one. A *drum sander* accessory for your drill will help you follow wavy or irregular shapes.

Steel Wool — a Safe Choice

Steel wool is the abrasive to choose when the furniture you are working on has a beautiful old patina or has been veneered. It's also great for general smoothing on irregular surfaces, such as carvings and turnings (on table or chair legs, for example).

SMOOTHING WITH A SCRAPER

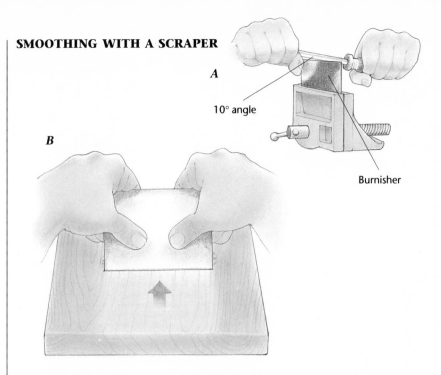

Scraping is an alternative to rough sanding. Form the scraper's hook with a burnishing tool or screwdriver (A). To use, bow the blade out with your thumbs (B).

Use the finer grades of steel wool, such as 2/0 and 3/0, and avoid rubbing too much in any one spot. Apply only light pressure to the surface and clean off any small particles of steel with a cloth moistened with paint thinner.

Synthetic finishing pads are ideal for cleaning up water-based strippers or rubbing down coats of water-based varnish or lacquer. Steel wool tends to rust or discolor these materials.

Scraping

Scraping is an alternative to sanding, and many woodworkers feel that the resulting surface is smoother and can take finishes better. Scraping is also handy for removing excess glue or finish and for reaching awkward spots and corners.

To scrape wood, all you'll need is a straight or contoured scraper, a burnishing tool, and two strong thumbs. The burnisher (some woodworkers substitute a screwdriver) forms the hook that makes the scraper work.

Burnishing an edge. First, file the edge of the scraper flat to smooth out any nicks or scratches. Next, polish the flattened edge on an oilstone or waterstone (skip this step for contoured scrapers). Finally, draw the burnisher straight down the edge a few times; then lower the burnisher's angle about 10° in each direction (see drawing above), and make several passes to shape the hook.

Using a scraper. Hold the scraper upright with your fingers behind, as shown. Bow the blade out with thumb pressure, rock the scraper away from you slightly, and push it along the surface of the wood. Getting the correct tension and angle is a matter of feel. Look at the wood you're removing: if you've produced sawdust, the angle is incorrect or the blade is dull; if you see minute shavings, you're on track.

A cabinet scraper, easier to use than a hand scraper, has a preset blade angle and a thumbscrew to control the amount of bow.

Color Control by Bleaching

Bleaching is the process of lightening the color of a wood by the use of chemicals. It's useful for removing or lightening color in specific areas (or on entire surfaces) before a new color is applied. Bleaching allows dark wood to be finished lighter. It can also remove dark stain that has not been completely stripped from previously finished furniture.

OXALIC ACID BLEACHING

1 *Mix oxalic acid crystals into hot water, stirring thoroughly, then brush over entire wood surface, working in line with grain.*

2 *As bleach goes to work, stains should begin to lighten. Wait until they fade or until solution dries; acid will revert to crystal form.*

3 *Don't sand or dust off crystals — they're toxic. Instead, wash wood thoroughly with wet sponge or rag. Finally, neutralize with vinegar. If stain remains or wood is blotchy, try rubbing surface with steel wool to even out color.*

The Three Types of Bleach

There are basically three types of bleach for use in woodworking. They are (from weakest to strongest) chlorinated liquid laundry bleach; oxalic acid; and commercial, two-part solution wood bleach.

Chlorinated laundry bleach is comparatively weak and is good for slight to moderate lightening. Repeated applications remove similar amounts of color, giving you some degree of control as you work on mottled or stained areas of wood. When used full strength, laundry bleach is effective for removing chemical, dye, ink, and other stains from wood surfaces.

Oxalic acid is the best bleach to use not only on many natural wood colors but also on many water and chemical stains. It's sold in crystal form at paint or hardware stores.

To prepare a standard oxalic acid solution, dissolve 3 ounces of crystals in 1 quart of hot water. For milder bleaching, oxalic acid may be used in a weaker solution.

Two-part bleaches are fairly expensive and very strong. Because of their strength, they can bring out really light tones on dark woods—something no other type of bleach can do. Unfortunately, two-part bleaches tend to obscure wood grain and figure, too.

Follow instructions closely and don't take shortcuts: potentially dangerous chemicals are involved. Since ingredients and instructions vary from product to product, follow the manufacturer's directions carefully and keep a close watch on the bleaching process. In a two-part bleach, the first liquid is often a caustic alkali; the second is usually strong hydrogen peroxide.

How to Apply Bleach

All bleaches are concentrated chemical solutions that can burn any skin or clothing with which they come in contact. When working with these chemicals, it's advisable to use rubber gloves, safety glasses, and a painter's mask, and to wear old clothes. If any bleach should accidentally get on your skin, wash it off at once with large quantities of water.

It's best to work outdoors whenever possible: not only does bleaching require good ventilation, but sunlight helps speed the process along.

Make sure that the surface to be bleached is smooth and free of grease, old finish, and wax. Since best bleaching results are obtained by uniform penetration, it is always a good idea to go over the surface with fine sandpaper to open the wood pores before you begin. And since all bleach contains water and will raise the wood grain slightly, you should be prepared to do more light sanding when the bleaching action is completed.

To apply bleach, use a synthetic-bristle brush (natural bristles are not compatible with the various chemical ingredients). Brush on any bleach in the direction of the wood grain to prevent unequal absorption and irregular lightening. Apply all materials evenly; don't try to saturate or flood the surface to speed the process along.

All chemicals, including bleach, leave some residue on the surface. Don't sand or dust off this residue: it's toxic. Instead, wash it off with a wet sponge or rag.

It's a good idea to neutralize the surface with vinegar. This step not only stops the bleaching process (and the smell), but keeps bleach residue from attacking subsequent stain or finish coats. Then rinse with clear water, wipe one last time, and allow the wood to dry thoroughly — about 24 hours if it's in a warm room.

SEALERS FOR SOFTWOODS

Generally, a sealer is applied to help protect the stain and wood filler as the finishing process continues. But put on at an earlier stage in the process, a sealer can also be used to tame the wild grain of some woods. On softwoods, applying a coat of sealer under stain will help the stain penetrate more evenly. This can minimize the mottled look stain can give to pine or soften the contrasting stripes it can create on fir plywood. It's also helpful to put a coat of sealer on end grain before a stain goes on, since this wood tends to drink up color at a faster rate and can look too dark if stained unsealed.

Shellac (see pages 64–65) is an effective sealer. Mix equal parts of 4-pound cut white shellac and denatured alcohol, then brush the mixture on quickly. After it dries, sand lightly with fine sandpaper and apply stain. Test the entire procedure on a hidden part of the furniture piece or on a scrap of the same type of wood. Try different ratios of shellac to alcohol to get the look you want.

You can also use commercial *stain controllers* (made specifically for sealing softwoods) or standard *sanding sealer.* Beware of synthetic (alkyd varnish) sealers, though: some are impervious to stain.

Stained pine (shellac sealer)   *Stained pine* (no sealer)

Stained fir plywood (shellac sealer)   *Stained fir plywood* (no sealer)

Coloring Your Project

Even though you've repaired your piece and sanded it smooth, it still may not be ready for the brush or spray gun. If you want the wood to have a clear, hard surface that shows off the natural grain, consider staining, sealing, and filling it before applying final finish coats.

A good stain gives color and a look of depth to the wood and enhances its natural beauty. And unlike a thicker surface coating, stain reveals much of the wood's original grain and figure. Older furniture may already have a rich patina; newer pieces, however, can often use a helping hand.

A sealer is to a clear finish what an undercoat or primer is to paint. It builds a surface to which the final finish will efficiently adhere and hardens the wood so it can stand up well to a thorough final smoothing. It also prevents stain and filler from bleeding through into subsequent top coats.

Fillers help level exposed surface pores on open-grain woods (such as oak and mahogany), enabling you to achieve a deep, glasslike finish, if you choose. A filler can be tinted to add additional surface interest.

There are many ways to decorate furniture, and more awaiting creative discovery. Applying a sequence of stain, sealer, and filler is the traditional way to emphasize wood's naturally decorative color and texture. For additional ideas, see Chapter 6, "Special Decorative Techniques."

Bold aniline dye stain is applied with foam brush; excess will be wiped off with soft cloth, allowing wood grain to show through. Jet black is added atop existing orange and red layers — one technique for creating custom colors all your own.

Staining

Many popular cabinet woods, such as mahogany, walnut, and other dark-colored species, frequently need no additional stain. They often look their best treated only with transparent oils or resins in a natural, clear finish. In addition, aged pine, maple, or cherry may already have a rich patina.

On the other hand, many light-colored woods — including new pine, birch, fir, beech, ash, oak, and poplar — can benefit from some form of stain by gaining more color and visual interest.

Stain, followed by an adequate clear finish, can be used by the finisher in at least four ways:

■ *Stain can give light-colored woods more character.* A golden oak stain, for example, can bring out grain pattern and pores of fine oak. Even a few darker woods, such as Philippine mahogany and walnut, sometimes need some form of stain to further emphasize their deep grain patterns and give them a richer appearance.

■ *Stain can give wood an "aged" look.* Pine probably illustrates this best. Putting a pine stain or wash on a new piece of unfinished pine furniture can add 100 years of artificial patina to the wood in about 15 minutes.

■ *Stain can make one species of wood look like another.* Tinting with an appropriate stain can make poplar, gum, and elm — all semihard, relatively plentiful cabinet woods with little, if any, natural color — resemble oak, mahogany, cherry, or walnut. (Grain characteristics of the original wood and the stained imitation are different, of course, but it often takes a trained eye to detect the disguise.)

SIX STAIN SAMPLES

Pigmented oil stains come in a full range of traditional wood tones; they're the most common stains on the shelves of hardware and paint stores. Gel stains are a new variation — even easier to apply than standard liquids. Penetrating oil stains combine color and finish in one step.

Pigmented oil
(golden oak stain on white oak)

Gel stain *(red mahogany stain on birch)*

Penetrating oil
(dark walnut stain on red oak)

■ *Stain can even out color from one part of a piece to another.* When you strip a piece, you may find it's composed of different grades — or even different species — of wood. Stain, either uniform or subtly varied in tone, helps smooth the transitions.

Which Stain Does What?

The chart on page 10 provides an overview of today's many options. Remember that your basic decision is between a *pigmented* and a *dye* stain. Pigmented stains are like thin paints, and lodge in pores and surface crevices. Dyes color wood fibers, and tend to be more brilliant and less grain-obscuring than pigmented stains.

Both pigments and dyes are available in a wide range of shades. Pigmented stains tend to supply the "wood-tone" range of colors, while dye stains also veer into intense shades, such as wine-red, green, and bright yellow.

Whatever type or color you're leaning toward, be aware that the small samples you see in stores and catalogs are only approximations of what you'll actually achieve on your project. Many factors influence the final effect. Among them are the specific wood's color, uniformity of grain (softer woods absorb more stain), and texture. New, unsealed wood will absorb more color than an older piece that's just been stripped.

Stain samples are often displayed on dense, uniform pieces of birch or oak; if they're on pine or fir, the samples have probably been sealed for more even penetration. To avoid surprises, test your choice on a sample of the wood you're using or on a hidden part of your furniture piece.

Five main stain types — pigmented oil, gel, penetrating oil, water (aniline dye) stain, and NGR — are shown below and on the facing page. A sixth sample shows wood that's been treated with pickling (referred to as liming, frosting, or antiquing) stain. Products for pickling are available in several forms; for more, see Chapter 6, "Special Decorative Techniques."

Dyes provide intense, even tones — they color wood fibers, not pores and crevices like pigmented stains. Water stains offer brilliant hues as well as wood tones. NGR stains don't raise grain. Pickling stains come in both pigment and dye versions, and combinations; choose them for convenient glazing, whitewashing, or "aging" effects.

Water stain *(wine-red stain on mahogany)*

NGR stain *(bright green stain on vertical-grain fir)*

Pickling stain *(slate-blue stain on pine)*

Staining

Successful Staining Techniques

Stain can be applied by a variety of methods, but most refinishers prefer to use a clean rag, paint brush, or foam brush.

Keep these thoughts in mind when you begin:

■ *Surface preparation* is the most important step in the staining process. Since a stain always highlights the surface to which it is applied, be sure your piece has been thoroughly sanded first; then go over the surface one more time with medium steel wool to be sure the stain is absorbed uniformly.

■ *Consider using a sealer* on end grain; this area is certain to over-absorb a stain (see "Applying a Sealer," page 53). Softwoods and fir plywood should also be lightly sealed (see page 43) so that, in spite of their uneven hardness, they can accept stain more smoothly.

■ *If you can't decide on the proper color,* start with a lighter rather than a darker stain. It is usually much easier to add color to a lightly stained surface than to lighten a darker one.

■ *Start on the least visible areas* of your piece, always checking to make sure that the stain's color, density, and absorption are what you had in mind. Your staining technique will get better as you progress.

■ *If you make a mistake,* use a commercial bleach (see pages 42–43) to remove the stain. Then start over again.

Apply a pigmented stain according to the manufacturer's directions. If you plan on using more than one can of stain, mix all the stain together in one large container first to ensure uniformity of color.

Pigmented stains, whether oil- or water-based, should always be stirred thoroughly before they are used. Unlike the dyes contained in other stains, the pigments in these settle to the bottom of the container

APPLYING A PIGMENTED STAIN

1 *Traditional pigmented oil stains need stirring before and during use. The pigments that contain the color are solids carried in oil. Gel stains, a modern variation, are ready to apply straight from the can.*

2 *Apply pigmented stains with a rag, a brush, or a foam brush. Using a rag, swirl the stain onto the surface, making sure to cover the surface quickly and completely. Don't worry about swirl marks or pileups of excess stain — you'll even these out later.*

during storage. These stains should also be remixed during use.

Brush or wipe the stain into the wood, as shown on the facing page (if you're wiping the stain on, use small, circular motions). Then wipe off the excess with a soft, clean cloth. Water-based stains typically dry faster, so you'll have to work efficiently to avoid lap marks.

If the color is too light, add more stain; if it's not quite right, you can try adding a different color. If it's too dark, you may be able to remove some pigment if you wipe immediately with paint thinner (oil-based) or a damp rag (water-based). The sooner you add more stain, the better, but don't expect a dramatic change: the crevices and pores are already saturated.

Let your furniture piece dry 12 to 24 hours before sealing and applying filler and/or a clear finish.

Apply a gel stain much as you would a traditional wipe-on stain. Shake the bottle to mix pigments, then squeeze some stain onto a clean rag. Wipe it onto the surface with long, even strokes; then wipe off the excess. Try to cover as large an area as possible at one time; recoat to darken the shade. Most gel stains dry faster than standard pigmented wiping stains — in about 4 hours.

Apply a penetrating stain in the same manner as a clear penetrating resin (see pages 62–63). Shake the can to mix the color; apply the stain with a clean rag; then use the same rag to remove any surplus oil and to equalize the surface color. Wipe the stain while it is still wet, after allowing enough time (brands vary) to ensure good surface penetration. Make sure the last strokes with your rag are parallel to the wood grain. Wiping across the grain may leave streaks, especially if the stain is too dry.

Because the color in most penetrating stains is fairly strong, they can look a bit blotchy, especially on softwoods. You shouldn't use a sealer or stain controller under a penetrating stain, however; penetrating stains are intended for use on bare wood. One solution is to choose a clear or natural penetrating oil and subtly tint it yourself (see "Custom Colors" on page 51) with universal

3 *Some pigmented stains can be wiped right off; others require a 10- to 15-minute wait. Use a clean rag and work in the direction of the grain, turning the rag frequently to pull off all excess stain. If you want a deeper color, a second coat may help.*

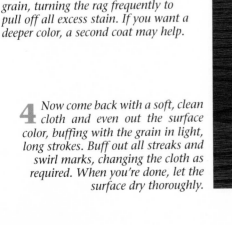

4 *Now come back with a soft, clean cloth and even out the surface color, buffing with the grain in light, long strokes. Buff out all streaks and swirl marks, changing the cloth as required. When you're done, let the surface dry thoroughly.*

Staining

or japan colors. Or try mixing a natural with a tinted version of the same product.

Apply a water stain only after experimenting on a piece of scrap wood — preferably of the same species as your furniture. Since water stains may dry lighter than the shade that first appears, let your test piece dry thoroughly before making any final color decisions.

Most water stains come in powder form. Dissolve them in hot water (some brands are first mixed with a small amount of methanol), let them sit, then strain to remove any undissolved particles.

To minimize raising of the wood grain when using a water stain, sponge the area to be stained with warm water. Lightly sand the surface before applying the stain.

A foam brush works well with water stain. Brush quickly onto the surface, making sure all surfaces are thoroughly coated (but not puddled); then wipe off immediately, using a clean rag (see photos below).

If the color is too light, you can recoat right away; if it's too dark, rub the surface firmly with a water-dampened rag. As shown on the facing page, you can change color by applying a new shade over the still-wet base stain, though each new shade will have progressively less effect. When you're through, buff the surface lightly with a clean white cloth, working in the direction of the grain.

A water stain will dry in 12 to 24 hours. Apply a sealer over the stain when it has dried. Then lightly rub the surface with very fine sandpaper to remove any remaining traces of raised grain.

Apply an NGR stain with a spray gun (see pages 60–61), if possible. Because these stains dry so quickly, they are difficult to paint on with a brush. If you must use a brush, add the manufacturer's retarder to slow drying time; or wash the area quickly with NGR stain solvent, then immediately brush on full-strength stain. When using the brush method, work as quickly as possible and be careful to avoid lap marks, runs, and other forms of unevenness.

APPLYING A WATER STAIN

1 *Aniline dye stains come in powder form; you mix them with hot water and — in some cases — a small amount of methanol. Stir thoroughly, let the mixture sit for an hour or two, then strain out any solids.*

2 *Foam brushes work well for spreading dye stains, but you can also use a standard brush, a rag, or even paper towels. Apply stain liberally to the surface, working quickly and making sure all areas are thoroughly covered.*

CUSTOM COLORS

What if you can't find a stain to match either the image in your head or the damaged tabletop in front of you?

Actually, your choices in color are practically limitless. A commercial stain is basically three things: color (pigment or dye), a vehicle (oil or water) that carries the color, and drying agents (solvents). If you understand the vehicle and solvents that deliver the color, you can choose from a wide range of compatible tones.

The simplest way to custom-tune stains is to mix two or more available shades from the same product line. Dye stains can be brushed on atop one another with fair success. With pigmented stains, it's best to fine-tune ahead of time.

Another way to go is to add color to an existing stain or filler. The art supply store is a good starting place: you can experiment with dried universal colors, japan colors, and artist's oils and acrylics. Paint stores may have tinting products as well — or try standard paint tints. Several mail-order sources (see page 14) stock universal and japan colors. All these products come in numerous shades, and can be blended to create many more. This is how many furniture repairers spot-match existing finishes. Just make sure the color-giver you choose is compatible with your base medium — naphtha, alcohol, lacquer thinner, or water.

Another option is to add the color to a final clear finish. However, tinted varnish, lacquer, or oil gives a more opaque look than does standard stain or (especially) dye. And tinting these finishes puts the color on the surface, not below it. As always, it's a good idea to test your experimental blends carefully.

3 *Immediately wipe off excess stain — leaving it on the surface won't make it much darker. Use a soft, clean rag and make final buffing in line with wood grain.*

4 *With water stain, you can mix colors in the container or, as shown below, by adding a second layer on top of the first. This is a red water stain over the orange base. You can also add a lighter second coat, but don't expect a dramatic change.*

5 *A third layer — this one black — has been added over the orange and red, then wiped off immediately. (Experiment on scrap wood first.) After buffing the surface, wait 24 hours before sealing, filling, or finishing.*

Green dye stain/blue filler   *Black dye stain/red filler*   *Cherry gel stain/walnut filler*

These three samples *show another coloring option: decoratively filled wood pores. Seal stain layer when dry, then simply color paste wood filler as desired and apply.*

Oriental chest *sports bright orange dye stain, plus several coats of clear lacquer on top. Black "hinge" details are really sprayed black enamel.*

DESIGN: AGNES BOURNE

Applying a Sealer

In wood-finishing lingo, "sealer" is a rather ambiguous term. It refers to any product capable of sealing (or partially sealing) wood surfaces. Sealer forms a solid bond between the wood and the top coat—much as a primer does with paint. At the same time, it puts a protective barrier over the stain and/or filler so the final finish won't get cloudy. And on medium- to closed-grain wood, sealer fills the pores so sanding can be more effective and finish penetration more even.

When to Seal a Surface

If you want to do a first-class job, you'll want to seal both the stain and the wood filler (see pages 54–55). Sealer coats, however, should not be applied so heavily as to give the pores no room to accept further finishing. Properly applied, a "wash" coat of sealer is invisible over a stain.

A sealer can lessen the effect of irregular grain in softwoods — especially plywoods — because it permits much more uniform distribution of stain. In such situations, apply the sealer before the stain (see page 43).

Which Sealer is Which?

Wood finishers have never completely agreed on the best type of sealer to use under successive finishing coats. One good solution is to use a thinned-down coat of your final finish, so product compatibility won't be an issue.

Shellac has been acknowledged for many years as an effective undercoat beneath lacquer, varnish, or more shellac. White shellac (see page 64) is used under light finishes, orange shellac under browns and mahoganies.

To prepare a shellac sealer for stain, mix 1 part of 4-pound cut dissolved shellac with 8 parts of denatured alcohol. For use over a filler, mix 1 part of shellac with 4 parts of alcohol.

If your final finish is a natural-oil varnish and you have no shellac on hand, you can make an excellent sealer by mixing 1 part of varnish with 1 part of pure turpentine. This will not work with synthetic varnishes (if the label indicates that your varnish can be thinned with turpentine, it is not synthetic). With synthetics, thin resin varnish with mineral spirits. With polyurethanes, penetrating resins, and most water-based products, you need no sealer.

You'll also find a number of *sanding sealers* on the market. As the name implies, these are effective for final sanding and have either a nitrocellulose (lacquer) or petrochemical (varnish) base that dries ready to sand in about an hour. Sanding sealers brush on easily, form a hard surface when dry, and contain an agent that makes the wood fibers stand up, permitting clean, powdery sanding.

Applying a Sealer

For best results, sealer coats should be as thin as possible. Brush on only one wash coat; sealer should flow onto the wood easily and dry quickly. Be sure to read the manufacturer's instructions on the label—application methods may differ with different brands. Smooth carefully when dry, using very fine sandpaper or grade 3/0 steel wool.

SEALER STEPS

1 Brush on thinned shellac, thinned varnish, or sanding sealer with quick, fluid strokes. You're not after a thick finish coat, just a wash atop the stain, filler, or bare wood. If you've chosen sanding sealer, make sure it's compatible with your intended final finish.

2 Let sealer dry (about 1 hour for shellac or sanding sealer, longer for varnish), then sand lightly with 320-grit or finer sandpaper or 3/0 steel wool. Simply smooth and clean the surface; excessive abrasion will wear through the sealer, possibly damaging the layer below.

To Fill or Not to Fill?

s a tree grows, its trunk retains a large amount of water. This water is stored in the pores of the wood but is lost when the tree is cut up for lumber and the wood is dried.

In oak, rosewood, mahogany, ash, walnut, teak, and other open-grain woods, the pores are large and very distinct. In closed-grain woods, such as pine, cedar, fir, redwood, birch, and poplar, the pores are very small and barely noticeable — but still open. Many other woods have pores that fall somewhere between these two categories.

No matter how carefully you have sanded and stained your piece of furniture, the wood pores will still be open and the wood surface not quite perfectly smooth. If you plan to give your furniture a penetrating finish (see "Easy-to-use Oils," pages 62–63), you'll probably want the pores to stay open; with this kind of finish, a natural look is part of the appeal. On the other hand, if you're refinishing an antique mahogany dining table, you'll probably want the deep, glasslike surface that comes only from carefully filling and then leveling the surface.

There are two ways to fill. The more time-consuming route, preferred by some finishers, is simply to apply coat after coat of finish until the pores are level with the rest of the surface. Or, to save yourself some work, you can use a wood filler before the final finishing coats. This method also gives you room for some creativity: you can tint the filler almost any shade you want, either emphasizing or contrasting with wood and/or stain color. (For examples, see page 52.)

Selecting the Right Filler

Fillers come in two basic forms: paste and liquid.

Paste filler is more common. It has the consistency of peanut butter, and must usually be thinned before it is ready to use. This type of filler is most suitable for such open-grain woods as oak, mahogany, and walnut.

The best paste fillers have a silex (ground silicate) base. They fill the pores in one application, do not change the wood color, and can be sanded to a smooth finish.

USING PASTE WOOD FILLER

1 *Thin or color filler as required, then brush liberally on the surface, stroking directly across wood grain. Rebrush again with extra pressure, forcing the filler into wood pores.*

2 *Wait a minute or two, then pull a plastic broad knife, putty knife, or squeegee along the grain, again driving filler into pores while cutting off surface excess. If you use a metal blade, be sure edges don't scratch the wood.*

Some paint and hardware stores carry paste fillers made with a cornstarch base. These are satisfactory, but may require several applications to fill the wood pores completely.

Paste fillers are usually purchased in a light creamy gray or "natural" color and then mixed, according to the manufacturer's directions, with small amounts of universal colors, japan colors, or pigmented oil stain to obtain the final desired shade. Premixed filler is also available in a number of colors.

It's usually a good idea to mix filler a little darker than the intended shade; all fillers lighten when dry.

Liquid filler is really nothing more than a thin sanding sealer containing a very small quantity of solids. Some finishers like to use liquid filler on maple, birch, poplar, and cherry. But most woodworkers don't

bother: if filling is required on these woods, they find it simpler to fill with extra finish.

How to Apply Filler

Before working with a paste filler, be sure it is thinned (according to the manufacturer's directions) to the appropriate consistency. Turpentine, naphtha, and paint thinner are standard thinning agents. The typical working consistency for filler is that of thick cream, though just how much thinning is necessary depends on the wood: the larger the pores, the thicker the filler should be. Stir paste filler thoroughly before and during use.

Apply filler liberally, using an old brush and working directly against the grain. Then work with the grain, using a knife or squeegee to force filler deep into pores. The surface will look terrible.

Allow the filler to set for 10 to 20 minutes, or until dull. Then begin wiping vigorously across the wood grain with a piece of burlap or other coarse cloth. This brisk wiping pushes the paste well down into the wood pores and at the same time removes any excess. Finally, buff the wood surface in the direction of the grain.

Let the piece dry at least overnight. When it's completely dry, sand the surface lightly in the direction of the grain to remove any last residue that may be lying above the pores. Leaving any filler on the surface could cause a streaked or cloudy effect in the final finish.

Although this step may be omitted, adding a last wash coat of sanding sealer or thin shellac is good insurance against the possibility of any paste filler's bleeding through into the finishing coats.

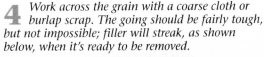

4 *Work across the grain with a coarse cloth or burlap scrap. The going should be fairly tough, but not impossible; filler will streak, as shown below, when it's ready to be removed.*

3 *Wait 10 to 20 minutes, or until surface filler glazes over, as shown above. Then immediately begin removing excess.*

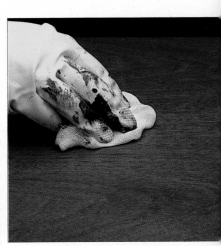

5 *Once excess material has been rubbed off, buff vigorously with a soft, clean cloth, working in line with grain. Let dry overnight, then smooth and clean surface lightly with fine sandpaper or steel wool.*

Applying the Final Finish

At last, you're in the homestretch: it's time to apply the clear or colored finish that will both highlight and protect your project. You can choose a subtle hand-rubbed penetrating finish, a glossy surface coating, or a good enamel with color punch. If you're confused about your options, be sure to read pages 8–11.

This chapter discusses traditional finishing procedures. For additional ideas, consult Chapter 6, "Special Decorative Techniques."

Be sure ventilation is adequate for the task at hand (see page 23), and be sure the air is warm enough: some finishes, especially water-based products, can be quite unpredictable at anything much lower than the ideal 70°F. For finishing, the drier the air in the work space, the better.

Always read the manufacturer's instructions on the container and check for any specific hints or precautions. But remember that the main requirement for a quality finish is quality prep work: sanding, staining, and/or sealing. In most cases, a finish won't hide flaws — it will magnify them.

Finally, if you want to rub down or wax your finished project to a custom sheen, turn to the special feature on pages 74–75.

Milky white when brushed from the can, nontoxic water-based varnish dries crystal clear. Three coats produce a tough, water-resistant finish. When dry, surface can be rubbed to high-gloss or mat sheen.

A Guide to Brushing & Spraying

 ost finishing materials discussed in this chapter may be applied either by brushing or spraying. Some, such as oils and penetrating resins, can also be wiped on with a rag.

Brushing is the most common and most economical method of applying a finish, requiring a minimum of setup and supplies. But brushing is much slower than spray finishing. Spray guns and the compressors or turbines that power them come in a wide range of shapes, sizes, and prices, and aerosol spray cans are handy for small projects. For guidelines on choosing brushes and spray equipment, see pages 13–14.

Whichever method you choose, brushing or spraying, make sure you are familiar with the principles involved before you begin your project. It *does* make a difference.

Proper Brushing Techniques

A successful brushing method is usually the result of combining common sense, good materials, and a little practical experience.

For starters, pour some of the finish from its original container into a larger one that's easier to use. A small plastic or metal bucket works well; so do wide-mouth "leftover" containers or microwave tubs.

Never dip the brush's bristles more than ⅓ to ½ their length into the finish — more finish than that will only work its way up the bristles into the ferrule and dry there, making the brush difficult to clean.

When withdrawing the brush from the finish container, don't drag the bristles over the container's edge to wipe off surplus finish. This practice adds air bubbles to the final finishing coat. Instead, slap the ends of the bristles against the inside of the container before removing the brush.

Brush all large surface areas; then fill in all brush strokes, moving with the grain. A brush held at a low angle lays on a smooth base coat; holding a brush upright allows you to feather with bristle tips.

Brush all turned table legs and other rounded shapes around their circumferences with light, lengthwise strokes whenever possible. Use the edge or tip of the brush to work the finish well into corners.

CLEANUP

It's a dirty job, but one that every finisher must face. Immediately after you use your tools, clean them. Don't delay — dried finish makes matters worse.

Use paint thinner to clean tools used with oil-based products; use lacquer thinner to clean up after nitrocellulose lacquer. Protect your hands with rubber gloves. Since you can't pour thinner down the drain or dispose of it easily, it's best to save and re-use it. Keep thinner in an old paint can or other container that won't be dissolved by the chemicals in the thinner. When thinner becomes very cloudy, let the solids settle to the bottom, pour thinner into another can, and dispose of the sediment.

It's not necessary to clean brushes and rollers if you plan to return to your project shortly. Brushes will keep for a few days if you hang them in the appropriate solvent; or wrap them in foil or plastic and put brushes used with oil- or lacquer-based products in the freezer and those used with water-based products in the refrigerator. Rollers or applicators will keep overnight in a plastic bag in the refrigerator.

Cleaning Brushes

Remove excess paint from a brush by stroking the bristles against cardboard; or put the brush between sheets of newspaper and press down while pulling out the brush.

Tools used with water-based or latex finishes are easy to clean. After removing excess finish (don't let it run down the drain), wash the brush with soap and lukewarm water, forcing water into the bristles and heel. Rinse the brush well.

To clean a synthetic- or natural-bristle brush used with alkyd enamel, varnish, or lacquer, work thinner into the bristles, especially at the heel. Then use a wire brush to get out

Synthetic-bristle brush

Each movement of your hand should be smooth and even as you draw the brush across the wood surface. If you press too hard on the bristles, you'll release too much finish. Lift the brush gently from the surface at the end of each stroke to ensure even coating.

On flat surfaces, brush the finish out toward the furniture's edges. This technique avoids ugly drips that can result when a fully loaded brush is pulled over a sharp edge. If you brush from lap mark to lap mark, you'll be incorporating the excess finish from one stroke into the new finish of the following stroke. Don't use unnecessary strokes: excessive brushing makes solvents evaporate faster, and your final result could suffer.

What if a loose bristle or dirt speck finds its way onto your newly brushed surface? Lightly poke it with a clean brush; it should stick to the dry bristles.

BRUSHING HINTS

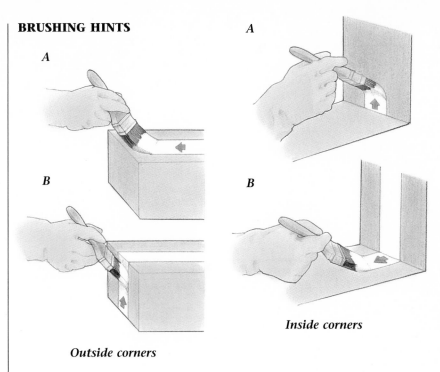

A

B

Outside corners

A

B

Inside corners

To brush outside corners (left), *first work outward to furniture edge, then pick up drips with the upstroke. On inside corners* (right), *brush upward from corner, picking up drips with the outward stroke.*

more finish. When the bristles are thoroughly clean, remove excess thinner by shaking the brush vigorously or tapping its handle against a hard surface.

After cleaning any brush, straighten the bristles with a bristle comb. When the brush is dry, wrap it in its original cover or in stiff paper or foil. Store it flat or hang it on a nail.

Bristle comb

Cleaning Yourself

Wet or dry water-based products are easy to remove from your skin; just wash with soap and water. Latex that has dried doesn't wash off clothing, however, so be sure to launder paint-encrusted clothes before the paint has dried completely.

A mechanic's hand cleanser will remove alkyd finishes. It's easier on your skin than paint thinner and just as effective. Use hand cleanser, not thinner, on any fresh alkyd finish that has landed on your clothing; then launder the clothes immediately.

Disposing of Finishes

If you bought too much finish and you don't want to store it, check the guidelines in your

area for ways to dispose of it. Some communities will accept paint for disposal one or two days a year.

If you have only a little finish left over, you can get rid of it by painting it onto cardboard and then discarding the dried cardboard (the ecological challenge is to prevent a liquid's eventual return to the water table). A good way to get rid of water-based finish is to solidify it by filling it with cat litter.

Wipe out paint buckets and roller trays with newspaper; let the paper dry before you discard it. Also let rags and empty cans dry thoroughly before putting them into the trash. Since finish- or thinner-soaked materials can catch fire, spread them outdoors until they're dry.

Brushing & Spraying

Spray-can Finishing

Though often more expensive than brush-on surface finishes, spray-on finishes are ideally suited for such intricate pieces as chairs, table legs, small novelty items, and louvered shutters. Spraying is also an effective way to apply a clear protective layer over a decorative treatment.

Unfortunately, many spray cans don't have sufficient power or a wide enough spray pattern to cover a large surface area. Another problem is that they normally contain only highly thinned finishing materials, which take longer to color and to build up a protective layer.

To avoid overspray, take special precautions to screen off your work areas and to protect all nearby surfaces. If you must do your spraying inside, use old bed sheets, newspapers, or plastic drop cloths to cover vulnerable surfaces. All aerosol finishes are highly flammable, so never use a spray can near an open flame.

It's important to hold the nozzle the proper distance from the surface — usually about 10 to 12 inches away. If the nozzle is held closer, too much finish will be applied, causing runs or sags. If the nozzle is held too far away, particles will begin to dry before they reach the surface and the resulting finish will be uneven. Try to work from a finished area into an unfinished area so that any overspray won't mar a previously finished surface.

To create a smooth, streak-free finishing coat, be sure that each new stroke overlaps ⅓ to ½ of the preceding stroke. Never end a stroke in the middle of your project: too much finish could build up, allowing runs or sags to develop.

After each use of your spray can, invert the container and press the nozzle until you're sure it is free of finish. Any finish remaining in the nozzle after use will dry, clogging the nozzle and preventing it from being used again.

Operating a Spray Gun

Techniques for using a spray gun are similar to those for aerosol cans. But nitrocellulose lacquer, the pro's favorite, requires a special spray booth, complete with exhaust fan, explosion-proof lights, and other materials specified by local building codes. New water-based lacquers are a much safer choice for home refinishers. For specifics on spraying lacquer, see pages 70–71.

If spray-gun finishing is new to you, practice various spraying techniques on an old cardboard box be-

SPRAY CAN DISTANCE

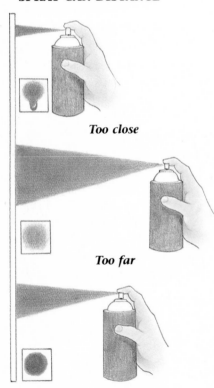

Too close

Too far

Correct distance

For best results, *hold spray can about 10 to 12 inches from surface. If can is too close, finish may run or sag; if it's too far away, surface will appear misty or sandy.*

THE FINISHING MOTION

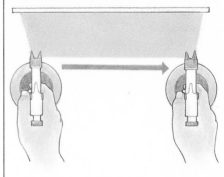

Correct

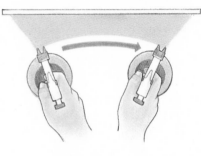

Incorrect

To apply finish evenly, *move spray gun or can parallel to work surface.*

fore you actually begin to apply finish to your furniture. Experiment with the full range of fluid and pressure adjustments available on your spray gun. Be certain to read any manufacturer's directions supplied with the gun, the turbine or compressor, and the specific finish you'll be using on your project.

Begin by moving the gun in long strokes parallel to the work surface, pivoting from your shoulder. If you move the spray gun only with your wrist, you'll "arc" each stroke, ending up with too much finish at the center of the stroke and too little at either end. The spray gun should be triggered before the beginning and end of each stroke to avoid buildup on the ends of the sprayed surface. The speed of each stroke should be about the same as if you were using a brush.

Try to keep the spray gun a consistent distance — between 6 and 10 inches — from the surface you're spraying. The closer the gun is to the surface, the more concentrated the spray of finish will be. Spraying close to the surface must be done rapidly to prevent runs and sags in the finish. When the gun is held too far from the surface, each stroke must be slowed down or the finishing material will not collect in sufficient density.

For professional spraying results, move the gun in straight, uniform strokes back and forth across the wood surface. Each new spray pattern should overlap ⅓ to ½ of the last spray pattern. By aiming each new stroke at the edge of the preceding stroke, you'll always get solid coverage without streaks, runs, or dry spots.

When you spray level surfaces, begin on the side of the piece closest to you and work toward its far side. This technique is especially important with lacquer, since lacquer overspray that lands on previously sprayed work will dry to a sandy texture. Since paint and synthetic finishes are also susceptible to overspray, plan a spray sequence ahead of time so you can avoid such problems.

When spraying flat surfaces, you'll often have to tilt the spray gun slightly. It's best to work at an angle of about 45° to the surface, with the spray gun at least half full. Whenever the piece itself can be tilted or set on one side instead, do so to minimize the need to tilt the spray gun.

If you don't want to spray certain parts of your piece, cover them with newspaper and masking tape before you begin. If you direct the force of the spray away from the

Before you begin, devise an orderly strategy that will minimize overspray. To finish a kitchen table, you might spray in this order: 1) inside surfaces of legs; 2) outside surfaces of legs; 3) outer edges; and 4) tabletop.

TACKLING CORNERS

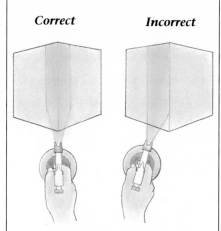

Correct   *Incorrect*

Spray all the corners first, *with spray pattern overlapping both sides of corner evenly.*

taped edge, a fine, even line will result. Remove tape soon after you finish spraying: it has a tendency to harden if it remains in place.

Finish all flat furniture surfaces, such as tabletops and dresser sides, by applying a band of spray to the

furniture's edges first and then spraying the center of the surface with long back-and-forth strokes. When finishing a table, begin by spraying the inner sides of the legs. Next, do the outer sides. Then spray around the outer edges of the table. Finally, spray the tabletop. You could reverse these steps, if you choose. The important thing is to decide on a specific finishing order before you start, so you minimize the chances of overspray on finished areas.

When you've completed the spraying, fill the spray cup half full with the correct solvent for the finish you were using. Use water to clean latex paints and water-based lacquers and varnish; use paint thinner or turpentine for oil paints or polyurethane varnishes; use alcohol for shellac; use lacquer thinner for nitrocellulose lacquer. Now all you need is an out-of-the-way place where you can spray the solvent out of the gun as you would a regular finish.

THE SPRAYING SEQUENCE

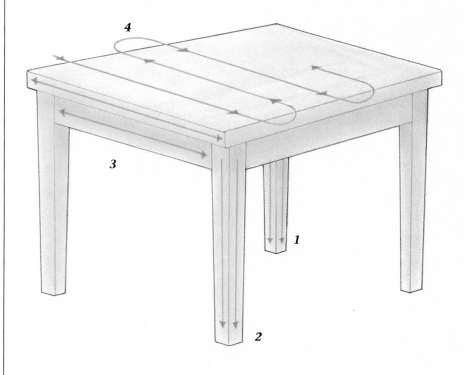

Easy-to-use Oils

Probably the finish first used on wood, oil is still one of the most popular treatments. Advances in paint chemistry in the last few decades have introduced a number of products that are oils by name, but which contain polymers, resins, and driers — giving them some of the properties of varnish and other more durable finishes. Traditional or modern, here are the choices.

Boiled linseed oil. Old-timers may swear by this penetrating finish, but the hours or even days it takes each hand-rubbed coat to dry, and the number of coats required, make linseed oil impractical for most projects. In addition, it's a rather soft finish that doesn't take kindly to water, heat, or chemicals.

If you do opt for linseed oil, dilute it with an equal amount of turpentine or mineral spirits and apply it sparingly with a brush or rag. When the wood pores have absorbed all the oil they can hold, wipe the surface briskly with a clean, dry cloth. After you feel that the "world's slowest finish" looks as beautiful as you had intended, wax or polish the surface for final protection.

To achieve nearly the same patina but in much less time, sandwich a layer of a good penetrating resin between applications of oil. As a first coat, oil enhances the color of the wood; as a second coat, penetrating resin protects the initial coating of oil; as a third coat, additional oil gives the wood surface the pleasant odor and natural feel of an old-fashioned, hand-rubbed finish.

Tung oil. This natural oil, built up in thin coats, produces a relatively hard finish that's quite resistant to abrasion, water, heat, acid, and mildew. Though its sheen increases with each coat, tung oil will never develop a high gloss.

Tung oil is often added to stains and varnishes. A true tung oil finish, however, should be either 100 percent tung oil or polymerized tung oil. The latter product combines pure tung oil with polymer resins and driers to produce a harder finish that requires less drying time.

It's best to thin 100 percent tung oil with mineral spirits — thick coats can wrinkle, obscuring the wood below. Rub the oil into the wood with a soft cloth. Apply at least two coats, 24 hours apart, then buff with a soft cloth or lamb's-wool pad.

POURING ON PENETRATING RESIN

1 *Apply penetrating resin with a rag or brush, or simply pour it on straight from the can. Don't worry about spreading it evenly — just make sure all surfaces are thoroughly covered.*

2 *Let resin sit for the prescribed time (typically 10 to 30 minutes), then wipe the surface clean. Come back with a soft cloth and buff out any remaining residue. Let the piece dry.*

3 *Multiple coats build sheen, especially if your resin contains a high percentage of varnish. Many refinishers apply additional coats with wet-or-dry sandpaper, rubbing fresh resin into previously applied layers.*

A hand-rubbed finish — whether it's oil, penetrating resin, or simply paste wax — gives wood a soft sheen and natural feel. The first coat fills the pores. Additional layers begin to build a richer look.

Penetrating resins. One reason these products are so popular is that they're so simple to apply. Commonly sold as *Danish oil, teak oil, antique oil,* or *penetrating oil sealer,* a penetrating resin preserves the feel of the wood and produces a relatively durable finish that can be easily patched or renewed. These products are essentially oil/varnish mixtures, and differences in relative proportions in the mix determine the differences in buildup and open (working) time between brands. In general, the more varnish, the higher the buildup from coat to coat; the more oil, the more slowly the product will dry.

4 *Another trick for final layers: burnish with steel wool dipped in a little bit of resin. Again, follow up each application by buffing with a soft, clean cloth. Paste wax helps protect the new finish.*

You can either stain the wood first (use a water-based aniline dye or a lightly pigmented stain to keep the pores from filling up) or use a tinted penetrating resin. *Don't* use a filler or sealer.

Be generous with your first application, called a flood coat. Apply the resin to the wood with a foam brush or rag, working on a horizontal surface whenever possible. Don't worry about brush marks during this application; you'll rub them out. Many furniture finishers don't even use a brush but simply pour the finish directly from the can onto the wood; then they spread the resin around with a rag or with a pad of very fine (4/0) steel wool. Wear rubber gloves.

Keep the surface wet for 10 to 30 minutes, depending on the manufacturer's instructions. If the surface begins to look dull, all the liquid has soaked into the wood and you need to apply more resin to keep it wet.

Wipe off the excess, then buff the wood with a clean, soft cloth. Some brands of penetrating resin are quite forgiving, but others turn to a sticky mess if you wait too long. If the coating gums up, dissolve it with more resin.

You can apply a second, third, or even a fourth coat if you want to build up the surface. Consult the manufacturer's directions for drying time between coats. Many finishers rub in these additional coats with wet-or-dry sandpaper — try 400-grit. (*Don't* use a power sander: liquids and electricity don't mix.)

For additional luster, rub a very dry surface briskly in the direction of the grain with 4/0 steel wool and a little resin. Wipe the surface clean, let it dry overnight, and follow up with a coat of paste wax, as described on page 75.

Classic Shellac

Long the standard by which other finishes have been judged, shellac is still one of the most beautiful wood coatings available. Though largely replaced by spray lacquer in commercial factories and by synthetic varnishes in smaller shops, shellac has held its own in the antique restoration and reproduction market. It is still the most popular finish for elegant French polishing (see page 66).

White (or "blonde") shellac is intended for light finishes. Orange shellac is suitable for browns or deep reddish shades — or for creating a "pumpkin pine" look on older pieces or reproductions. You may also find brown (or "button") shellac, an unrefined product similar to 17th- and 18th-century finishes. Samples of all three types are shown below.

Shellac comes in either flake (dry) or liquid (dissolved) form.

Hardware and paint stores typically stock white and orange shellac in liquid form. Flakes or buttons are available from specialty shops or by mail (see page 14).

Buying and mixing shellac. Shellac deteriorates with age. (White shellac, typically sold dissolved in denatured alcohol, has a shelf life of only 3 to 6 months.) For this reason, always buy liquid shellac in small quantities from a dealer with enough turnover to ensure fresh stock.

If you have doubts about the shellac's age, test it on a piece of scrap lumber. If it takes a long time to dry or remains tacky, it should not be used.

With a supply of longer-lasting flakes on hand, you can simply mix up as much liquid shellac as you need for a particular job. The amount of flakes you add to a gallon of alcohol determines the strength of the shellac, measured in *cuts*. A 1-pound cut is made by dissolving 1 pound of flakes in 1 gallon of alcohol; a 2-pound cut uses 2 pounds of flakes to a gallon; and so on. If you've never worked with shellac before, begin with a 1-pound cut — it's thinner and more forgiving of mistakes.

Liquid (dissolved) shellac is typically sold in 3- or 4-pound cuts, for economy. To make a 1-pound cut from a 4-pound one, add 3 parts alcohol to 1 part shellac.

Applying shellac. Shellac is not a one-coat finish. You must build up a surface with several coats before the finish begins to take on luster. But because shellac dries dust-free in 15 to 30 minutes and can be applied again within an hour or so, the entire finish can take as little as a day to complete.

Begin by brushing on an even coat of shellac, using a brisk but smooth motion. Take special care to overlap all adjoining brush strokes and to maintain a clean, smooth surface. This will help keep ridges and streaks to a minimum. We found foam brushes ideal for laying on shellac, though some brush manufacturers discourage this use.

After an hour or so, rub or sand off the high spots with 320-grit sandpaper or 4/0 steel wool. The shellac should sand to a powder. If it clogs the paper at all, wait a few more minutes before continuing.

Apply a second coat the same way as the first. Sand it down after another hour of drying.

The third coat should be smooth enough for rubbing. If not, sand one last time and apply more shellac. Then use 4/0 steel wool and lubricating oil to even up the surface gloss. If you're after a high-gloss look, allow at least 3 days for the new finish to harden; then rub and wax, as detailed on pages 74–75.

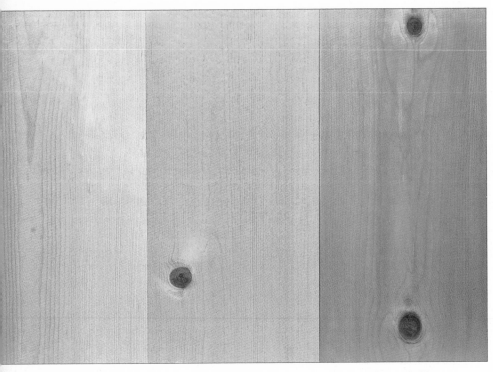

White shellac　　　*Orange shellac*　　　*Brown shellac*

SHELLACKING A DRESSER

1 *Buy shellac premixed or mix your own (it's often fresher). To make a 1-pound cut, dissolve 16 ounces of flakes in 1 gallon of denatured alcohol (or 4 ounces of flakes per quart).*

2 *The key to a successful shellac job is to apply many thin coats instead of one or two thick ones. Work quickly, letting shellac flow onto the surface smoothly and evenly.*

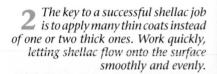

3 *Let shellac dry for about 1 hour, then sand lightly with 320-grit sandpaper or steel wool. If shellac has dried properly, it will turn to powder as you sand.*

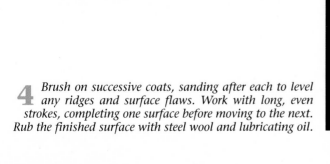

4 *Brush on successive coats, sanding after each to level any ridges and surface flaws. Work with long, even strokes, completing one surface before moving to the next. Rub the finished surface with steel wool and lubricating oil.*

FRENCH POLISHING

The luxury of a French polish finish — multiple, ultrathin coats of shellac — has traditionally been found on only the most cherished antiques. Favored for use on Louis XIV, Chippendale, Sheraton, and Hepplewhite furniture, French polish was valued not only for its beauty but also for its practicality. No other finish can equal its tough but velvety sheen. And no other finish can be as easily repaired.

Since any French polish finish requires a fair amount of time and energy, it's usually not practical for today's commercial furniture. But for the home craftsman who wants to refinish an antique or who has already invested many hours making something carefully from scratch, the extra time French polishing takes is well worth the effort.

Though traditional methods call for white shellac and a lubricant such as paraffin oil, mineral oil, or boiled linseed oil (see photos below), modern woodworkers often substitute commercial padding lacquers with good results. Some traditional finishers add ground pumice to the mix as a combination filler/polisher, while others omit this step.

If the wood in your chosen project needs staining before finishing, it's best to use water-based aniline dye stains; other types may lift during the extensive rubbing the French polishing process requires. As with any finishing procedure, practice on scrap wood before you start to work on a treasured antique.

Make French polishing pad (above left) by first forming gauze, cotton, or cheesecloth into a small ball. Then lightly wrap core with a piece of lint-free cotton or linen.

Squeeze pad against palm (above right) after you dip pad lightly in boiled linseed oil and then in 4-pound cut of shellac; the squeezing mixes the two finishes together.

Pad shellac/oil mixture gently onto wood (left) without stopping. Work quickly to cover entire area, being careful to blend each padding stroke with the next. Many finishers begin with broad figure-eight strokes, gradually switching to tighter circles and straight lines. Repeat shellac/oil applications.

Durable Varnish

Varnish is probably the toughest, most moisture- and heat-resistant finish with which you can protect your furniture. Even though a good modern varnish takes longer to apply and to dry than shellac or lacquer, its durability makes it the preferred choice for many home woodworkers.

Available in gloss, semigloss (satin), eggshell, and flat sheens, varnishes vary widely in their characterists. Alkyd varnish and polyurethane are two main varieties; three spin-offs are phenolic-resin (spar) varnish, rub-on varnish, and water-based materials. For a description of each type, see the chart on page 10.

Here are application tips for alkyd varnish, polyurethane, and rub-on mixtures. For a closer look at water-based finishes, see page 69. Apply exterior spar varnish in the same manner as interior alkyd products.

Applying alkyd varnish. Often referred to as oil-based varnish, this is the most common of the new interior types. (*Natural* varnishes, increasingly scarce, are mixed in turpentine.) Though not as hard as polyurethane, alkyd varnish is more flexible, so you can recoat without worrying about bonding.

Because alkyd varnish is thinned with mineral spirits, it's compatible with most stains, fillers, and sealers. Like most varnishes, it's susceptible to darkening with time, but can be stripped with chemical removers.

Fillers are seldom used with varnishes, but a sealer is always recommended. It's simplest to use a thinned-down solution of the varnish itself as a sealer. Build up the surface with gloss varnish, then switch to the sheen of your choice for the final coat.

*A **varnish finish** supplies both a warm glow and great protection; it's an especially good choice for elegant dining ensembles like this one. The final finish may be rubbed out to either a high gloss or a soft satin sheen.*

DESIGN: HIRO MORIMOTO ASSOCIATES

Durable Varnish

Since varnish remains tacky for 2 to 6 hours, dust is its number-one enemy. Pick a clean work space and vacuum all surfaces a few hours before setting up. Make sure the room is warm enough — air temperature can make a big difference in drying time.

Avoid runs and drips by not overloading your brush and by keeping the work horizontal when possible. It's particularly important to apply varnish sparingly — you can always add more later.

Don't stir varnish too vigorously, or it will become bubbly; in fact, only semigloss or flat varnish needs to be stirred at all.

Apply varnish with smooth, continuous strokes, working in whatever direction is easiest. Is the surface totally covered? Complete the process by stroking lightly along the grain, this time using only the tips of the bristles (see photos below).

Use the fewest brush strokes you can, and work only on one small section at a time. This will allow you to finish the piece section by section, without creating lap marks. Side-lighting the work will help you avoid dry spots. If you find one later, don't go back — just try to cover it with the next coat.

After letting the varnish dry at least overnight, use 320- or 400-grit sandpaper to remove the gloss and provide better adhesion for the next coat. Once the final coat is completely dry, you can rub the surface lightly with 4/0 steel wool for a mat finish or with pumice, rottenstone, or polishing compound for a higher gloss (see pages 74–75).

Applying polyurethane varnish.
The ultimate in resistance to abrasion, moisture, heat, and chemicals, polyurethane is in some ways a "miracle finish" for tabletops, floors, and other high-use areas. Though it's somewhat brittle, it's extremely popular because of its toughness. Another consideration: once this finish has cured, it's permanent — no solvent will dissolve it, and new coats won't bond to it chemically.

Never use polyurethane as a sealer for anything but a polyurethane top coat, and don't put it over shellac, lacquer, or most enamels.

Careful surface preparation is a must with polyurethane; otherwise, the finish tends to "skid" across the wood. Whenever possible, choose a stain that is guaranteed to be compatible with the final finish; check the manufacturer's label to be sure. You probably won't need a filler — polyurethane fills pores on its own.

Brush on one to three coats of gloss polyurethane, using light strokes to avoid the "dipped-in-plastic" look this finish sometimes produces. Try not to let more than 24

BRUSHING ON ALKYD VARNISH

1 To apply varnish, first brush it on in any direction, wetting the entire surface. It's a good idea to apply a thinned-down sealer (see page 53) before full-strength coats.

2 Immediately come back with relatively dry bristles in line with the grain, "tipping off" the varnish with light, smooth strokes. Most brush strokes will level as they dry.

3 Let varnish dry overnight, then sand lightly with 320- or 400-grit sandpaper. Sanding levels dust nibs, minimizes brushing mistakes, and provides good bite for the next layer.

hours elapse between coats; otherwise poor adhesion may result. Scuff the wood between coats with 220-grit abrasive paper or 3/0 steel wool to level the surface and provide better bite for the next layer.

If you would rather not leave the surface glossy, use 320-grit wet-or-dry abrasive paper and water or 4/0 steel wool and oil to rub the finish down to a dull glow. Or, if you prefer, you might apply a coat of satin polyurethane over the last gloss application.

Rub-on varnish. This penetrating resin-and-varnish mixture is rubbed in like a penetrating resin (see page 63), but because of its higher content of solids, it builds up in layers on the surface. Each coat increases the sheen.

With a rub-on varnish, you trade durability for ease of application. Like other penetrating finishes, it darkens wood. It's irreversible on open-grain woods.

4 *Apply a second layer in the same manner as the first — against the grain, then tipping off with the grain. Two coats may be adequate; if not, apply a third. If desired, switch to satin, eggshell, or flat sheen on the final coat.*

WATER-BASED VARNISH

New water-based varnish goes on milky white (above left), but dries hard and clear (above right).

One of the most promising new developments for the home finisher is the availability of better water-based clear varnish and lacquer. These "alternative" finishes have been around for some time, but the new generation of products is much improved. The new compounds are tough, they give good coverage, and they look great. Besides being better for the environment, better for your health, and easier to clean up (you just use soap and water), these products have several other distinct advantages. They dry much faster than standard varnish, they level nicely, and they stay very clear.

But water-based finishes take a little getting used to if you're accustomed to standard oil-based varnishes and polyurethanes. Though they dry clear, they have a disconcertingly milky appearance in the can and when brushed on (see photo above left). Don't try to work this whiteness out; it will disappear on its own. Apply water-based varnish like standard varnish — laying it on, then tipping off with a very upright, relatively dry brush.

Water-based products *do* raise wood grain, but it's a straightforward matter to pre-wet the surface and sand off surface nibs. Easier still, just wait until after the first coat has been applied and use 220- or 320-grit paper. Fish eyes (tiny bumps in the surface) can also be a problem; if they plague you, look for a product made by a manufacturer that also supplies fish-eye eliminator. Water-based finishes are very sensitive to temperature — your work area should be as close to 70°F as possible.

Most water-based varnishes build up a little more slowly than resins, and you'll probably need three coats instead of two. To seal knotholes or to provide a little traditional amber color, you might try a coat of white or orange shellac as a sealer.

Water-based finishes dry in about 4 hours — as opposed to 24 for traditional varnish. Smooth between coats with a synthetic finishing pad (steel wool may leave specks of rust). Wet-or-dry sandpaper and varnish-impregnated tack cloths may cause their own problems: they can leave oil or wax films that produce fish eyes. If you use them, clean the surface carefully before top coating. Wait several days before using the finished piece.

Fast, Dust-free Lacquer

Clear lacquer is a favorite of professional woodworkers. If it's sprayed on, it dries within seconds, eliminating the dust problems associated with varnish and other surface finishes. You can lay down several lacquer coats in the time it takes a single application of most other finishes to dry.

Though neither as tough nor as moistureproof as varnish, a lacquer finish is durable and can be rubbed to a high gloss. Lacquer is more heat- and chemical-resistant than shellac, and shares the same quality of invisible layering (each additional coat softens — and bonds to — the previous one).

If you're working with open-grain wood, don't expect lacquer to fill the pores. Use a filler and follow it with a lacquer-based sanding sealer.

Most lacquer available on the market today is nitrocellulose that's been dissolved in solvents. However, newer water-based lacquers are gaining popularity fast. They're not only far less explosive and noxious, but they also provide clear, tough finishes.

You can buy lacquers for spraying or brushing. Though the nature of the products is essentially the same, the solvents and thinners in brushing lacquer evaporate more slowly, so brush marks have a little more time to level out. Don't try to apply a spraying lacquer with a brush unless the manufacturer offers a retarding additive specifically for this purpose.

Both types of lacquer are generally available in gloss, semigloss, and flat finishes. Many woodworkers prefer to use gloss lacquer for its superior strength and clarity, then dull it when dry by rubbing (see pages 74–75).

Spraying lacquer. You'll get the best results if you use high-quality spray equipment (see pages 13–14). You can rent a gun and turbine or compressor from a paint store or tool rental outlet. Be sure to follow any directions supplied with the equipment.

Spraying nitrocellulose lacquer, which may not even be legal in your area, requires a carefully constructed spray booth for safe application. Nonflammable, nontoxic, water-based lacquers are thus far more practical for home spray finishers.

Still, it's best to set up your project outdoors or in a well-ventilated, out-of-the-way indoor spot to prevent overspray from spreading beyond a limited area and to keep dust off your work.

LACQUER: SPRAY IT OR BRUSH IT

1 *Spraying is the easiest — and fastest — way to apply lacquer. Aerosol cans are handy for small projects, HVLP spray guns for large ones. Unless you have a formal spray booth, work outdoors — or use only water-based products.*

2 *Build a lacquer finish slowly, sanding lightly between thin coats with 320- or 400-grit sandpaper. You won't need to wait long — sprayed lacquer is ready to sand in about an hour. Each new coat melts the one below, providing a firm bond.*

Brushing lacquers *offer an alternative to spraying. Apply thin coats, waiting about 4 hours between applications. Choose a product specially formulated for brushing, or add a compatible retarding agent to the spray formula.*

DESIGN: PETER AND DIANE HURD

Clear lacquer *goes on quickly and is very versatile. Mahogany-and-satinwood piece at left has 12 lacquer coats, each hand-rubbed with steel wool to a soft glow; tabletop detail above shows depth of this classic gloss finish.*

The usual finishing procedure requires two coats of sanding sealer, followed by two or more coats of lacquer. You smooth between coats with progressively finer grades of wet-or-dry sandpaper, beginning with 220-grit on the sealer and ending with 400-grit before the final lacquer coat. (For spraying techniques and tips, see pages 60–61.) After 24 hours, you can rub the final surface to either a mat or a gloss finish.

An alternative for small projects is to use spray lacquer sold in aerosol cans. This method produces good results but requires many coats, since the lacquer is thinned greatly so it can pass through the can's nozzle.

Because of environmental concerns, spray cans containing nitrocellulose lacquer are no longer sold in some areas.

Brushing lacquer. Brushing lacquer will also produce a first-rate finish, but you'll need to work quickly, and you'll need to sand carefully between coats.

Whether you choose a gloss, semigloss, or flat lacquer, you may want to build up the underside of the surface with gloss because of its strength and clarity. The final coat can be semigloss or flat, or you can add a flatting agent to your gloss lacquer. Even with gloss lacquer, you can create a mat finish by scrubbing the final coat down with fine steel wool.

For best results, always thin lacquer according to the manufacturer's instructions. Never work with lacquer that won't flow easily.

Begin by brushing the lacquer onto the wood in a smooth coat. Working rapidly with a wider than normal brush to speed things along, spread the lacquer with long strokes without too much back-and-forth brushing. Keep your working areas small, and finish one area at a time. Pad applicators (see page 13) work well on large areas.

Even though the surface will dry dust-free in minutes, the key to success is to wait at least 4 hours before sanding or applying a second coat. Then carefully level any high spots or defects with 320- or 400-grit sandpaper.

Apply additional coats until you build up the finish you desire (two coats over a sealer is a bare minimum). After the final coat has dried overnight, you can rub the already shiny surface with rottenstone, polishing compound, or 600-grit wet-or-dry sandpaper for an even higher gloss.

Applying the Final Finish **71**

Enamel: Cover it with Color

For bright color, or for masking lower grades of wood, choose enamels. They're available in flat, semigloss, and gloss finishes, and in a wide range of colors. The higher the gloss, the tougher the coating — and the easier the resulting surface is to clean.

Enamel choices. Enamels are essentially clear finishes (lacquers or varnishes) with pigments added. Here are the four basic types:

■ *Alkyd-based enamels.* These paints have an oil base and use paint thinner as a solvent; their characteristics are similar to those of alkyd varnishes. The finish produced is both flexible and durable.

■ *Latex (water-based) enamels.* Also called acrylic or vinyl enamels, colored latex varnishes are odorless, nonflammable, and easy to apply. Their big advantage is water cleanup. But they're not as durable as other enamels and won't produce as much gloss.

■ *Polyurethane enamels.* Like polyurethane varnishes, these enamels have good resistance to abrasion, but are somewhat brittle. They can be employed for both interior and exterior projects. Use paint thinner for cleanup.

■ *Colored lacquers.* These enamels can be identified by searching the label for nitrocellulose content. Colored (or pigmented) lacquers provide a durable and beautiful finish. Like clear lacquers, they're available in spray or brush form. Aerosol spray cans are handy for small projects (but are unavailable in some areas). Spray-gun application, the pro's choice, requires an approved spray booth.

Applying enamel. Always begin your paint job with an undercoat, or primer. Not only does the undercoat seal the wood, it also serves to point up any remaining surface flaws, which can then be patched and sanded. For bare wood, use either pigmented shellac or an alkyd primer, applied with a brush or roller. After priming, smooth the surface with 220-grit sandpaper.

When repainting an enameled piece, don't bother to strip the finish. Instead, use the existing paint as a primer, simply patching and sanding the surface smooth.

Brush enamel generously onto the wood, then feather it out with lighter strokes in the direction of the grain. Another technique useful for large areas is to lay on the paint with a 3-inch roller, then smooth it out with light brush strokes. Or use a pad applicator.

Let the first finish coat dry for at least 24 hours. Sand with 320- or 400-grit sandpaper before you apply another coat. For a finish with remarkable depth and clarity, make the last coat clear varnish (or put two coats of clear lacquer over colored lacquer).

PAINTING: TWO TECHNIQUES

Don't bother to strip an old finish off — use it as a "primer" for new paint. Simply patch as required, sand the surface smooth with 220-grit sandpaper, and apply a new enamel coat.

A 3-inch paint roller makes short work of large expanses. This is a two-step process: first roll on a rather thick coat of enamel, then top off lightly with a relatively dry brush to remove roller marks.

When enameling, *there's no law against having fun. Hallway bench (left) and canvas were both decorated with leftover paint; grand piano (below) took on vibrant new life with colored spray lacquer. For a host of other decorative techniques, see pages 76–95.*

73

RUBBING & WAXING

Rubbing and/or waxing can lend elegance to a finish, whether it's oil, shellac, lacquer, varnish, or enamel. Done with one of several fine abrasives, rubbing removes brush marks, dust, and lint from the finish so the surface reflects light uniformly, with full sheen. Waxing adds depth and luster, and at the same time protects the finish.

Rubbing

You'll need both a lubricant and an abrasive for rubbing. The tra- ditional lubricant is paraffin oil, but almost any kind of oil, or even water (except on shellac), will do. The lubricant is spread in a thin film over the surface of the wood.

For a mat finish, the tradi- tional abrasive is ground pumice. Buy FFFF, the finest grade, and shake it on sparingly (an old salt- shaker works well). If you prefer a glossier finish, choose tradi- tional rottenstone. Rub either of these abrasives across the lubri- cated surface, using a felt block, blackboard eraser, or cork sand- ing pad. Keep your strokes long and even, and rub in the direc- tion of the grain.

If an auto supply store is closer than a hardware or paint store, you can substitute automo- tive rubbing compound for the pumice or rottenstone — many pros do.

Another method of rubbing is to coat the surface with water as a lubricant, then sand with wet-or-dry sandpaper, using small squares of very fine grit (600 or finer) wrapped around a felt- or rubber-lined sanding

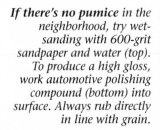

Tried-and-true rubbing method (above) involves working ground pumice into newly oiled surface. Paraffin oil is shown, but other lubrication would serve as well. A felt block or black- board eraser is great for rubbing. Pumice kept in old saltshaker is easy to apply.

If there's no pumice in the neighborhood, try wet- sanding with 600-grit sandpaper and water (top). To produce a high gloss, work automotive polishing compound (bottom) into surface. Always rub directly in line with grain.

block. This will produce an even mat finish, but it can be improved by buffing with a lamb's-wool pad attached to an electric drill. To produce an even higher gloss, apply automotive polishing compound after the initial sanding.

Once you've rubbed the entire surface, wipe off the slurry that has formed and check the surface for any spots that still gleam. Keep rubbing until they're gone. Complete the job by wiping off all traces of the lubricant, using a soft rag.

Waxing

Wax is inexpensive, easy to apply, and easy to renew. You can make your own by dissolving pure beeswax in turpentine until a soft paste forms. However, this wax won't be as durable as commercial floor or furniture paste waxes, which contain varying amounts of carnauba wax (a much harder product with a higher melting point). Some products are tinted for use on dark woods; these may help mask scratches or wear spots.

Spoon the wax onto a moist cotton sock or rag, then fold the cloth around the wax to make an applicator. Knead the cloth with your fingers to distribute the wax evenly.

Rub the wax into the finish, using large, circular motions. Apply just enough to create a thin film — excess wax will dull the surface and leave it gummy.

Let the wax dry until it hazes over (about 10 to 20 minutes), then buff with a soft cloth or with a power buffer fitted with a felt or lamb's-wool pad.

Wax adds luster and protection to any finish. Spoon paste wax (below left) onto moist rag or sock to make applicator for wax coating. Then rub wax evenly over wood surface (below right), pushing it deep down into any open wood pores.

Polish newly waxed surface (above) with a soft cloth or power electric buffer fitted with felt or lamb's-wool pad.

Special Decorative Techniques

Decorative finishing is a great way to jazz up an inexpensive piece of unfinished furniture or bring new life to a battle-weary relic. But don't try it on something old and valuable; this technique is for flea-market finds. Many decorators consider it a badge of honor to spend the absolute minimum on a chest or chair to be revived with paint: that's part of the fun.

Some decorative effects mimic aging. Some reproduce traditional styles. And others are purely abstract. Pickling and antiquing are traditional methods for recreating the look of a hard-won patina; stenciling, striping, gilding, marbling, and graining are also time-tested techniques. Popular treatments like sponging, ragging, and spattering can add a wash of fresh color, subtle or bold, to a tired surface. There's no right or wrong in decorative finishing. Techniques are as varied as the imaginations of the finishers.

Remember, though, that decorating furniture is not the same as finishing furniture. The decoration itself provides little protection for the wood surface. But putting a coat or two of a clear final finish over the decorative treatment can usually give the wood all the protection it needs.

Colorful chest showcases several decorative techniques: serpentine marbling on top, plus a golden glaze overlaid with hand-painted vines on the bottom. Drawer pulls of oxidized copper complement both top and bottom colors.

Before You Begin

Brushing or rolling a solid coat of paint onto a surface produces a neat, opaque finish. But take the same paint, thin the color and consistency a little, and apply it in translucent layers with a brush, sponge, or other implement, and you've created a look with new depth and vitality.

Such surface painting is sometimes rather imprecisely called a faux finish. Technically, however, the term refers to a finish that simulates something real (*faux* means "false" in French). Some decorative finishes do trick your eye into thinking you're looking at real wood, marble, or stone. But this type of painting needn't mimic a particular substance. It can simply be an abstract interplay of colors, or some other product of your imagination.

Most decorative painting techniques use tinted washes and glazes (see facing page) to build up rich, glowing layers of color. For additive techniques — such as sponging on, ragging on, and color washing — you simply add color. For subtractive techniques — such as antiquing, sponging off, ragging off, dragging, and marbling — you add color, then remove some of it so that the background shows through.

Choosing a Technique

If you don't have much experience painting, try one of the easier techniques first, such as sponging on, ragging on, color washing, or stenciling with a precut pattern. Sponging off, ragging off, and dragging are a little more difficult. Marbling and graining require real skill.

Some techniques, such as dragging and marbling, look best on a smooth surface, since they tend to make any flaws more noticeable. Sponging and ragging on are appropriate for bumpy, irregular surfaces, since they camouflage imperfections.

Or play up the age of the piece by pickling or antiquing — and/or additional distressing.

The Base Coat

Depending on the condition of your piece and the decorative medium you're using, you may need to apply a base coat. An eggshell finish is usually recommended for this. Water-based coatings — latex washes and acrylic glazes — adhere best to a latex flat or eggshell base. They don't stick well to a glossier finish, even if it's deglossed.

Oil glazes will adhere to flat or low-luster latex or alkyd base coats. You can even use an oil glaze over a semigloss or gloss finish if you sand first.

Most paints are designed to be used over some type of priming agent. It often isn't necessary to prime an existing finish that's in good condition, but you may want to repair any nicks or scratches before decorating. Don't forget to rough up a glossy surface by sanding it, whether you're priming it or painting directly over it. If the existing surface is not in good condition, you may need to strip it (see pages 23–25), repair it, and prime it again before recoating.

For bare wood, use either pigmented shellac or an alkyd primer, applied with a brush or roller. This primer should cover the area completely, but doesn't have to be as neat as finish coats. Smooth the primed surface with 220-grit sandpaper.

Tools for decorative painting include (1) bristle-softening brush, (2) graining brush, (3) synthetic stenciling sponges, (4) artist's brush, (5) standard paintbrushes, (6) natural sea sponge, (7) comb, (8) stencil brushes, (9) fan blender, (10) mottling brushes, (11) feather, (12) artist's brushes, (13) cork, (14) pencil overgrainer.

Washes & Glazes

Most decorative painting techniques involve the use of washes or glazes. Technically speaking, a wash is watered-down latex paint, and a glaze is oil-based or acrylic color thinned to translucency.

Since washes dry quickly, they are suitable for simpler techniques, such as sponging. The more complex techniques — those requiring a buildup of color, such as marbling — are best accomplished with glazes, which stay wet longer and give you more time to manipulate them before they dry.

Oil- or water-based? Oil glazes, the traditional medium of decorative painters, stay wet and workable longer than either washes or acrylic glazes and produce a wonderfully translucent finish. Mistakes are easy to correct: you just dab on paint thinner and wipe off the paint. Note, however, that handling oil-based paints and paint thinner requires caution because of the chemicals and fumes involved.

Acrylic glazes and latex washes are easy to use, since they're mixed and cleaned up with water. Although water-based compounds don't generally last as long as oil-based ones, you can always apply a clear coating to protect the decorative treatment.

Making washes and glazes. It's not difficult to mix your own wash or glaze. Just follow the instructions and recipes at right.

Washes are extremely simple to prepare. All you do is add water to ordinary latex paint.

To make a glaze, it's easiest to start with a transparent commercial glaze — basically, paint without pigment (sources for commercial glazes are listed on page 14). Then add paint from a paint store — alkyd for an oil glaze, acrylic for an acrylic glaze. The intensity of the color will be thinned by the commercial glaze, resulting in a kind of translucent paint.

You can also use paint from an art supply store or crafts shop. Japan colors and artist's oils are compatible with oil glazes, artist's acrylics with acrylic glazes or latex washes. Use universal colors to tint any medium.

First blend paint with a small amount of glaze, then add remaining glaze. To the colored mixture, add the appropriate solvent—paint thinner for an oil glaze, water for an acrylic glaze. The solvent dilutes the paint so that it can be applied in very thin coats. To extend the drying time of an acrylic glaze slightly, you can add a retarding agent.

The recipes below are just a starting point. Decorative painting isn't an exact science. In fact, it's more akin to cooking than to chemistry. Don't be afraid to experiment as you become more practiced and confident.

Transparent Coatings

A clear coating over a painted surface protects the finish, makes it washable, and can give it sheen. If you want to finish with a clear coating, look for a non-yellowing, water-based one (see page 69) that can be applied over any finish. Such products are available in both satin and gloss finishes.

Recipes for Washes & Glazes

Latex wash

You can vary the ratio so that water makes up from 10 to 90 percent of the mixture. The more paint you use, the more durable the finish.

> *1 part latex paint*
> *2 parts water*

Oil glaze

A good general recipe for beginners, this glaze stays wet even if you work slowly. For faster drying and a harder finish, use less commercial oil glaze and more paint thinner.

> *1 part commercial oil glaze*
> *1 part alkyd paint*
> *1 part paint thinner*

Acrylic glaze #1

This glaze recipe is suitable for ragging, sponging, and simple marbling. Change the proportions to 5 parts commercial acrylic glaze, 1 part paint, and 1 part water for techniques requiring greater translucency, such as dragging, graining, and more sophisticated marbling.

> *1 part commercial acrylic*
> *glaze*
> *2 parts acrylic paint*
> *1 part water*
> *2–4 oz. retarder per gallon*
> *(optional)*

Acrylic glaze #2

Use this recipe if you don't have easy access to a commercial acrylic glaze. Look for acrylic gel medium in an art supply store.

> *1 part acrylic gel medium*
> *1 part acrylic paint*
> *2 parts water*
> *2–4 oz. retarder per gallon*
> *(optional)*

Pickling

Pickling, liming, frosting, whitewashing: all these terms refer to the technique of applying thin paint — either white or pastel — over bare wood (such as pine, birch, or oak), then wiping it off before it dries completely. The pigment lodges in any nooks, crevices, or knots, leaving the rest of the wood surface slightly lightened. Pickling works well on unfinished pieces; it's often less effective on older, previously finished pieces, unless they're intentionally distressed.

When it comes to pickling products, the choice is broad. You can use an acrylic or oil glaze, a commercial pickling stain, or ordinary latex paint thinned with water.

Before pickling, you may wish to emphasize the texture of the surface by brushing it with coarse steel wool or a wire brush, working in the direction of the wood's grain. This is the time to add any intentional dents, holes, or "wear" spots (see below).

Brush a thick coat of wash onto the piece and let it dry slightly. Then begin wiping, starting in the center of each flat surface and working toward the outside edges, wiping with the grain. Wipe the paint away from high spots, but leave some in the surface indentations. Also try to leave

DISTRESSING

When furniture is "distressed," it is artificially aged or worn. Distressing is a way to give instant history to new, unfinished furniture, as well as to impart a time-honored look to wood that shows few signs of ever having been used.

You can imitate the look of wear and tear on furniture by using practically any hard object — a rock, an old nail, a heavy tool, or a chain. Simulators of antiques use knives, rasps, and abrasives to make wear marks, rough grinding wheels and key chains to produce nicks and gouges, and small drills or nails to mimic the effect of wood-boring worms.

Distressing is often combined with other decorative treatments, such as pickling or antiquing. Or brush on layer upon layer of enamel and/or glaze, then selectively sand through, exposing color coats below.

Since distressing is not a finishing technique, be sure to apply a clear coating over your work.

Here are a few suggestions for ways to give furniture a pleasingly timeworn appearance:

■ *Worn edges,* probably the most obvious signs of age in furniture, can be simulated with the use of files, rasps, and sandpaper. Any worn spot you add should be placed in an area that would naturally receive high use. Your treatment could suggest a corner rounded from years of moving, a chair rung flattened by many shoes, and so on.

■ *Worm holes* can be simulated with small nails, drill bits, ice picks, or even a shotgun blast of birdshot at 30 feet. Or try spattering (see page 86) with dark paint. Such holes are most often found around the legs of tables and chairs — the first places where hungry worms might enter.

■ *Dents* in the surface can be made by heavy stones, keys, chains, or a small hammer. Make sure you use a blunt object, though — you don't want to tear the wood fibers.

DECORATIVE PAINTING: CROWORKS OF MARIN

some of the wash in corners, on edges, and in molding details to accent and add depth to the final finish. Is the color too faint? Apply it again, this time using thicker paint or a longer drying time. Too thick? You may be able to remove more of the color if you wipe it with the appropriate solvent.

Because a pickled surface is so thin, it's easily damaged. It's best to seal a pickled piece with a clear, non-yellowing surface varnish or lacquer. Or, for a flatter antique look, simply buff with a paste wax (see pages 74–75).

PICKLING A ROCKER

1 *First scrub piece with a steel brush and sandpaper to open pores, adding distress marks if you wish. Then brush on latex wash (about 1 part water to 2 parts paint) as shown.*

2 *Once wash begins to set, simply wipe some away, using a damp sponge, cloth, or dry brush. Paint will lodge in pores and cracks. For additional color, repeat the process.*

■ *Dark spots, rings, or burns* are easy to reproduce. Use a propane torch and wire brush, or do it the real way — by staining with ink or placing a hot pot or casserole right on the surface.

With a little imagination, the resourceful furniture finisher can create many other distressed effects. When you've made all the surface dents and abrasions you want, lightly sand any rough edges to give the marks a more natural appearance.

Painted chest (facing page) received numerous color coats, which were sanded through to expose layers below. Farm table (right) and matching chair were carefully distressed, antiqued with blue paint, and accented with painted and gilded designs.

INTERIOR DESIGNER: SHARON CAMPBELL; DECORATIVE ARTIST: ROBERT O'CONNOR

The Art of Antiquing

ntiquing a piece of furniture really just consists of applying a thin glaze of one color over a base coat of another color. The glaze is lightly wiped away as it dries, so the base color shows through, creating a slightly two-tone effect. Also known as toning, shading, or glazing, antiquing is especially effective on inexpensive unfinished furniture or over poor-quality or distressed surfaces.

Though usually associated with enamel, glazing can also be applied as stain over stain (especially useful for highlighting carvings) or even as a veil of color between coats of clear varnish.

A major advantage of applying an antique finish is that it often eliminates the need for removing the old finish. As long as the existing finish is in good condition, you simply need to clean it well with detergent and water and wipe it with denatured alcohol to eliminate excessive wax buildup.

Consider most blemishes or dents in the old finish to be assets: they'll catch a larger share of the glaze coat and stand out, giving a highlighted, gracefully worn look. You can also inflict a little abuse yourself, using any number of common household items; for details, see "Distressing" on pages 80–81.

Applying the Base Coat

If the existing finish is in good condition, you may already have an excellent base for antiquing. If a new base is needed, prepare the wood thoroughly and apply the base as you would any regular enamel.

Applying the Glaze

Once the base coat has dried, brush the antique glaze liberally over the surface, working the finish into cracks, corners, molding details, and blemishes or "character" marks in the base coat. Concentrate on one small, manageable section at a time. When the wood has been thoroughly

covered, start gently wiping away excess glaze with a soft cloth, working in line with the grain.

Be sure to wipe the glaze away from high spots, but leave some in surface indentations. Also try to leave some of the glaze in corners, on edges, and in details to accent and add depth to the final finish.

Making an Impression

After the glaze has been lightly wiped to your satisfaction, there are a number of other techniques that will let you obtain an even more unusual finish. Three of these — dragging, imprinting, and color washing — are discussed below. Always practice these tricks on scrap wood before trying them on your furniture.

Dragging. Dragging, or combing, consists of creating thin stripes on a surface. First you apply a glaze or wash to the surface (a glaze is easier for beginners); then you drag downward with a brush or other tool to

ANTIQUING AN END TABLE

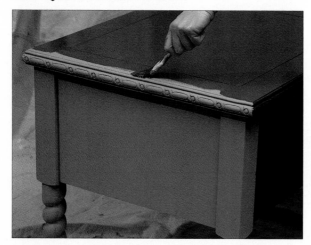

1 Brush oil glaze on top of base coat — we used about 1 part each commercial glaze, alkyd paint, and paint thinner. Don't worry about how it looks; just work plenty onto the surface.

2 Then remove most of the glaze, wiping evenly along wood grain as shown — or using any of the techniques shown on the facing page. Let excess glaze remain in any depressions, carvings, or corners.

open narrow stripes of the background color.

The pattern can be neat and uniform or rough and irregular, depending on the dragging tool you use. A brush is traditional; you can buy special dragging brushes, but an inexpensive paintbrush will do as well. Or you can use cheesecloth; a comb sold for decorative painting; or a device you make yourself, such as a squeegee in which you've cut notches. It requires speed to drag a large section before it dries, as well as some care to keep stripes parallel.

Imprinting. Brushes, rags, and sponges aren't the only materials you can use to make intriguing patterns in furniture. You can press into service any number of items found around the house, such as waxed paper, plastic wrap, paper bags, burlap, or a feather duster.

You'll find that it's easier to make impressions in a glaze rather than in a wash, since a glaze stays wet longer. If you're working with a nonabsorbent material, such as waxed paper, you'll need a plentiful supply, since glaze will build up rapidly on it.

Color washing. One of the simplest decorative techniques, washing consists of building up very thin layers of translucent color for a rich, warm glow. You can use glazes, latex washes, or undiluted latex paint.

Generally, the thinner the coat you apply, the richer the result. You can use variations of the same color or different but related colors. Applying a lighter-colored glaze over a darker one will give a chalky, aged effect. Use a darker glaze over a lighter one to produce a glowingly translucent quality.

The effect you get also depends on the tool you use and how you manipulate it. Blend an oil glaze with a dry cotton rag or piece of cheesecloth; or use a large, dry paintbrush. Try a clean, damp sponge or paintbrush on quick-drying latex.

THREE GLAZING OPTIONS

To drag a wet glaze, position a large, dry paintbrush at top of strip and press hard so that bristles bend back to heel of brush. Drag brush down length of surface without stopping. Wipe brush on a rag after each pass.

Crumpled waxed paper also creates an intriguing pattern in wet paint. Other common items, such as plastic wrap, trash bags, burlap, or a feather duster, also have possibilities.

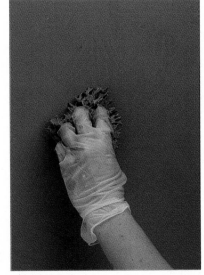

Color washing builds thin, blurred layers of related colors. Here, a natural sea sponge is used to smear on and push around undiluted latex top coat in irregular patches.

Sponging

The easiest faux technique for a beginner involves using a natural sea sponge to make mottled impressions on a surface. You can *sponge on* (sponge one or more colors onto the wood) or *sponge off* (use the sponge to remove wet paint).

Sponging off generally produces a more subtle effect than sponging on. For either method, you can use a latex wash or glaze; or, for sponging on, try undiluted latex. If you decide to use a latex wash for sponging off, thin the paint only slightly, instead of making the standard wash.

The look you achieve depends on the colors you select. A pastel color over an off-white background will produce a bright, cheery effect; a dark color over a light background will create a bold, dramatic look; variations of the same color will give the surface an impression of depth. When you sponge on more than one color, the color you apply last will dominate. Sponging looks best on large furniture pieces, though not on those that are intricately carved.

The effect you get also depends on the type of sponge you choose and the way in which you wield it. A large, flat sea sponge is best for this technique. If you have a round sea sponge, cut it in half to get a flat surface. Medium-size pores are preferable: small pores produce a fussy pattern, and large pores create a coarse look. The sponge imprints look most effective when they're applied over the surface randomly but with uniform pressure. Be sure to keep changing the position of the sponge as you work.

Look for sea sponges in home decorating and art supply stores, in bath shops, and in cosmetic departments of drugstores and health food stores. Ask for a wool sponge rather than a grass one.

SPONGING ON A GRANITE PATTERN

1 *Apply base coat and let dry. Then wipe undiluted latex paint sparingly onto damp sea sponge. Dab surface lightly as shown, rotating sponge when you lift it to vary the pattern you're creating. Leave space for additional layers, if you choose.*

2 *Let entire sponged surface dry completely. If desired, apply a second color, following same procedure. Here, light gray latex goes over the black. Undiluted latex creates durable finish.*

3 *For corner areas and details where sponge will not reach, use a fine artist's brush to make dots simulating mottled impressions of sponge. A third sponged layer has been added — the same taupe color as base coat. Repeat color adds depth to surface.*

Ragging

A relatively easy technique for a beginner, ragging consists of pressing a soft cotton rag onto a wet surface to make a textured impression.

You can *rag on* (apply one or more colors to the surface with a rag) or *rag off* (use the rag to remove wet paint). A latex wash or a glaze is suitable for either technique, though it's much easier to rag off a glaze, since it stays wet longer than a wash. A latex wash is ideal for ragging on.

The effect you achieve depends both on the type of rag or other material you choose and how you maneuver it. A soft cotton cloth absorbs the glaze or wash well, is easy to manipulate, and doesn't show hard edges when it's pressed against the surface. Old cotton napkins and new T-shirts are good choices. (Avoid old, tattered T-shirts — the fabric may not hold enough paint for effective ragging.)

Just be sure the cloths you choose are clean and lint-free, and plan to use the same material throughout the procedure. Cut the material into 1½- or 2-foot squares, making sure there are no frayed edges.

It's easy to vary the effect of ragging. Simply change the pressure you're using on the rag, roll it around on the surface, or rearrange its shape occasionally as you're working.

Again, the result depends on your choice of colors. For a dramatic look, select bold, contrasting colors, such as red on a yellow background; for a softer effect, use quiet or pastel colors; to achieve a sense of depth, try variations of the same color. No matter how many colors you use, always let some of the background show through.

Once the surface is dry, protect it with clear varnish or lacquer.

RAGGING ON

1 Immerse a clean, dry, lint-free rag in first wash or glaze and wring out well. Then loosely bunch up rag and press lightly on surface. To vary pattern, rebunch and rotate rag as you work. When color begins to fade, reload rag.

2 Let entire ragged surface dry completely. If desired, apply a second color, following same procedure.

3 Let second ragged color dry completely. Apply a third color, if desired. Final result should be an attractive blend of colors.

Spattering & Stippling

Sponging, ragging, and antiquing are fun, inexpensive ways to beautify worn-out or downright ugly pieces. If it's dots you're after, you may want to consider two other techniques: spattering and stippling. Both are illustrated at right.

Spattering

Here you shower a base coat with flecks of contrasting paint. To cause the shower, just hit the handle of a loaded paintbrush against the handle of a dry brush or stick held perpendicular to the brush; or flick the bristles of the loaded brush with your fingers.

Spatter on as many different colors as you like; just let each one dry before you apply the next. For small, fine flecks, dilute the paint — but not so much that it runs.

When all spattered layers have dried, seal the surface with a clear, protective finish.

Stippling

While spattering is an additive process, stippling is subtractive: you reorganize a wet glaze into a mass of dots. Since this decorative pattern is subtle, it's more effective to use bold colors for both the glaze and the background.

After brushing on a glaze, you dab the surface with the tip of a dry brush. Special stippling brushes are expensive, but you can also use an ordinary stiff-bristled paintbrush, a stainer's brush, a scrub brush, or even a toothbrush.

You can also lightly stipple a freshly glazed surface with either a dry sponge or a wadded paper towel. Applying crumpled newsprint to the wet glaze often results in a pebbly, marbleized surface.

SPATTERING & STIPPLING DETAILS

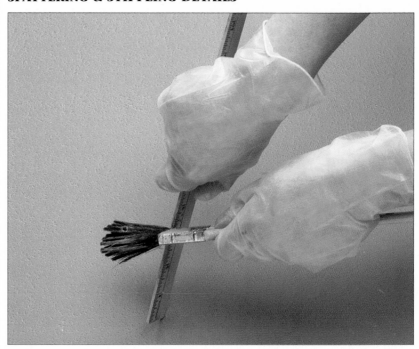

To spatter *a piece, rap the handle of a loaded brush against a stick or dry brush.*

Stippling *rearranges a wet glaze: you dab the surface with a dry stippling brush or other tool.*

Graining

Although truly realistic copying of a specific wood's grain pattern is an art that requires years of practice, you might want to give it a try. Even if the finish you create doesn't fool a botanist, it can still be very pleasing.

Mahogany Graining

Traditionally, grainers have chosen expensive, exotic woods, such as mahogany, to copy. Mahogany has two main types of grain: arched heartwood and straight. You can simulate either with a brush called a fan overgrainer. For a special treatment, mask off a central panel framed by rails (horizontal pieces) and stiles (vertical pieces).

Ask the paint store to mix a color that duplicates the rich, warm hue of mahogany. Or do it yourself, mixing equal parts of burnt sienna, alizarin crimson, and raw umber, using artist's acrylics in an acrylic glaze. Some professionals paint over a dirty pink base coat; others like a reddish yellow background. Finish with a clear glossy coating.

Fantasy Wood Finishes

Creating a fantasy grain doesn't demand as much practice as imitating authentic wood grain, and can lend almost the same appeal.

If you apply a dark brown glaze over a background of pale yellow, you'll get a fairly realistic look. But you can just as well use reds, blues, or any other colors that strike your fancy. Similar colors work well together; apply the darker shade over the lighter one. To create the look of a wood's grain pattern, use a pencil overgrainer or other instrument, such as a cork. Once the glaze is dry, apply a transparent coating to the surface to protect it and give it luster.

MAHOGANY GRAINING

1 *After brushing on glaze, flog wet surface (pat with flat of a brush using quick, bouncing motion), always working away from yourself. Here, masking tape defines a central wood "panel" inside rails and stiles.*

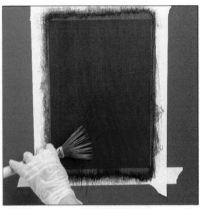

2 *To simulate mahogany heartwood, make a series of arches, using a fan overgrainer. Dip brush into paint, dabbing off excess; then spread bristles with fingertips. Hold brush nearly parallel to surface and at a right angle to arches you're creating.*

3 *Blend grains wih a bristle-softening brush held at a right angle to surface.*

4 *With fan overgrainer, make a straight grain at a slight angle on one side of arched heartwood; repeat on other side.*

Marbling

Marbling options include the traditional but tricky glaze method and a simpler but less subtle process using latex washes. Both techniques are described below.

With either glazes or washes, you can copy a specific type of marble, if you wish, or create your own impression of marble. A flat, self-contained surface like a tabletop makes a good starter project. Don't try to marble ornately detailed pieces if you're a beginner.

Marbling with a Glaze

Working with a glaze, the traditional method for marbling, requires a bit of practice and a good sense of timing — the surface must be neither too wet nor too dry.

The technique consists of applying a tinted glaze over a nonporous background, building fields of color, and creating a network of veins over the surface. You then soften and blur the design before applying the final veins. (Plan to complete an entire small area before starting on a new one.) Finally, the thoroughly dry surface is covered with a transparent coating to give it a uniform sheen and to protect the finished design.

Marbling with Latex Washes

It's also possible to create an interesting marbled surface using latex washes. The advantage here is that the procedure doesn't require the same sense of timing needed for marbling with a glaze, since each wash layer dries quickly.

Working on a surface with a solid-color background, you build up layers of color and veining. Use a natural sea sponge to dab on latex wash in irregular shapes or drifts. Then blot the wet surface with a clean, damp sponge to spread drifts and soften them. Add veins with a feather dipped into thinned latex paint or artist's acrylics. Each layer that you add blends and softens the previous layers.

DECORATIVE ARTIST: SHELLEY MASTERS

MARBLING WITH A GLAZE

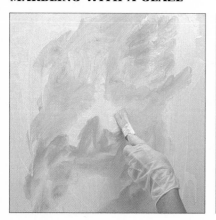

1 On small area (no more than 6 square feet), brush on a background glaze to match color of marble you're creating.

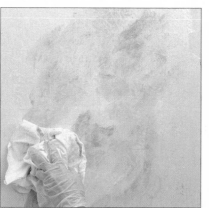

2 Using additional glazes in other colors, paint irregular shapes, or drifts, over wet surface. After applying each glaze, rag it off (blot with a dry, bunched-up rag — see page 85). Expect some blending of colors.

3 Put a dab of paint (artist's oils for oil glaze, artist's acrylics for acrylic glaze) on one side of brush tip; holding dry side of brush against surface, make veins, using a light, shaky motion. (Paint from other side will come through.) Blot veins with a dry rag.

__Tabletop__ highlights both marbling and graining techniques. Marble drifts are fashioned with acrylics, sealed with water-based varnish.

__Chess, anyone?__ Game board squares alternate light and dark marbling effects. Border is faux malachite; fashion patterns with comb, wire brush, or torn edge of stiff cardboard.

DECORATIVE ARTIST: SHELLEY MASTERS

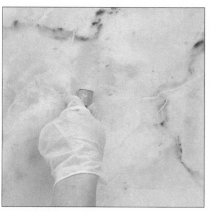

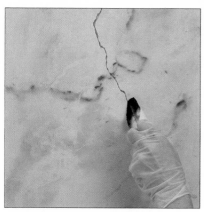

4 *Wait several seconds for glaze to dry slightly; then soften and blur it lightly with a blending brush held at a right angle to surface or with crumpled tissue paper. If you blend when glaze is too wet, you'll smear or streak it.*

5 *Make additional veins by scraping through glaze with edge of a cork, using a squiggly motion. Blot veins with a dry rag or crumpled tissue paper, or soften them with a blending brush.*

6 *Apply a small amount of thinned paint (use a color that will stand out from others) to a fine liner brush or to tip of a feather. While supporting your elbow with your free hand, make final veins with a light, shaky touch. Continue to next small area.*

Stenciling & Lining

One of the simplest and most inexpensive ways to decorate a surface, stenciling allows you to express your individuality in a colorful and lively way. Simple edge lining is also straightforward and can add a touch of individuality to either traditional or contemporary pieces.

Stenciling

Use a precut stencil or make your own (instructions appear on the facing page). Your design may call for adding a single color or two or more colors. It's best to stencil over sealed, bare wood or over a flat, eggshell, or satin finish — the paint you use for stenciling won't adhere well to a glossier surface.

STENCILING A CHAIR BACK

1 *Place first stencil carefully, then dab the surface with stencil sponge dipped in undiluted artist's acrylics. Stencil over either sealed wood or glazed or opaque base coat.*

2 *This is the third layer: white goes atop previously applied red and purple. Index marks help alignment, prevent confusion. White is also used to undercoat yellow (fourth layer), a relatively weak pigment.*

3 *A fifth layer — green — completes the design. Touch up any smudges with a damp rag or with an artist's brush and base coat color. Then protect your creation with a sealer coat of varnish.*

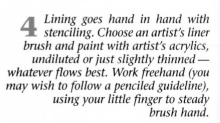

4 *Lining goes hand in hand with stenciling. Choose an artist's liner brush and paint with artist's acrylics, undiluted or just slightly thinned — whatever flows best. Work freehand (you may wish to follow a penciled guideline), using your little finger to steady brush hand.*

You can use ordinary latex paint for stenciling, or choose paint from an art store. Among artist's paints, the easiest to use are artist's acrylics, which are water-soluble and provide intense, quick-drying color. Although japan colors dry instantly, they're flat and require paint thinner for mixing and cleanup. Artist's oils, also soluble in paint thinner, are extremely difficult to use for stenciling since they dry very slowly and smudge easily. Regardless of which type of paint you use, it should have a thick, pasty (not runny) consistency.

If your stencil repeats, measure the width (or height, for vertical placement) of the surface to determine how many repeats will fit. Arrange the designs from the center of the surface out to the edges so corners will match. You may want to reduce the space between designs so they'll be complete at the corners.

To apply the paint, use either a small-celled synthetic sponge or a short, blunt-bristled stencil brush; you may find a sponge easier to manipulate than a brush.

Lining

If you look around, you'll notice that decorative lines or stripes are far more widely used on furniture than you might have expected. Although intricate spider-web designs are difficult to accomplish without a certain amount of practice, simple edge lining — the major kind used on furniture today — is fairly easy to do. If you use an artist's liner brush (sable works well), you can draw a variety of different lines simply by turning your wrist and changing the angle of brush to surface.

The key to lining is a measured, controlled pace. Use the little finger on your brush hand (see photo on facing page) as a guide, or steady the stroke with your free hand. If you make a mistake, simply wash off the offending acrylic, let the surface dry, and try again later.

MAKING YOUR OWN STENCIL

Although the selection of precut stencils is wide today, you may want to make your own — perhaps to match or coordinate with a decorative element already present in the room, or to carry out a particular theme. Fortunately, you don't have to be an artist for this job, since it isn't necessary to create the design yourself. You can copy a design you like or trace one from a book of stencils. If the prototype isn't the right size, simply enlarge or reduce it on a copying machine.

Clear acetate (.0075 or .010 gauge) is the easiest material to use for stencils. You can layer as many sheets as you need to and still see the original design clearly. You can layer up to four sheets of mylar (.005 gauge), but you won't be able to see through them as easily.

Each color should be on a separate stencil, unless the sections that are to be painted in different colors are spaced far apart. You'll also need separate stencils if the design has many small elements running close together, even if they're the same color.

Transferring the design. Draw the design to the desired size on graph paper. If you're copying from a stencil book, the design will already have bridges — narrow strips that link the parts of the design and keep the stencil from falling apart. Otherwise, you must put in bridges yourself by breaking the design into logical segments and placing bridges there. Color the completed design with appropriately colored pencils or markers so you'll know which shapes to cut on each stencil.

Trim the stencil material to the size of the design, leaving 1-inch margins on all sides. Tape the first piece of stencil material over the design and trace the areas that will be painted in the first color, using a technical pen and India ink (on mylar, use a felt-tip pen). If your design involves more than one stencil, leave the first in place and tape additional ones on top.

To make index marks on each stencil, trace a section of the design with a dotted line. Don't cut on this line; use it for aligning the new stencil with the pattern.

Mark the top front side of each stencil, and number the stencils in their order of application.

Cutting the stencils. Place the stencils, one at a time, on a flat, firm cutting surface. Using a utility or craft knife, cut the stencil, drawing the knife toward you in a smooth, continuous movement. When you're cutting curves, turn the design rather than the knife. Trim any jagged edges. Don't worry if the cut edges aren't perfect: slight flaws will not be noticeable in the finished work.

If you have a clear photocopy of the design in the exact size required, you don't need to draw the design on the stencil material. (Note, however, that you will have to draw in bridges if there aren't any in the design.) You can simply tape the photocopy to the stencil material and use it as a cutting guide. You'll need a separate photocopy for each color in the design; use a colored pencil or marker to fill in each color.

Computer stencils. If you have access to a personal computer, drawing software or scanner, and a laser printer, you might also fashion stencil designs on the screen — then simply print them onto acetate and cut.

Painting Patterns

A battered but beloved old chair and a stark, unfinished new dresser might both benefit from surface decoration in the form of bold stripes, diamonds, or other geometrical shapes. There are no rules: simply view the furniture piece as if it were a three-dimensional canvas.

Buy fast-drying acrylics in any colors you like. Crafts stores sell 8-ounce bottles in a range of shades. If you have a large surface to cover or require custom-mixed tints, a paint shop is the best source, though the smallest size sold there is 1 quart.

For professional-looking results, your wood surface must be as close to flawless as possible before the color goes on. After careful sanding, apply a coat of acrylic gesso in an even layer, using 1 part water to 4 parts gesso; smooth out any lumps with a dampened brush. Let dry 1 to 2 hours, then sand again. Repeat once or as many times as you like.

For some designs, you may want to outline your pattern on the gesso in pencil, then fill in the color or employ a resist method, using masking tape to block out some areas and define others.

When you paint, start with the lightest color, using tape or contact paper to block out areas adjacent to where you want that color to go. Repeat as your design requires. Let acrylics dry for at least 24 hours before you fix them with a clear sealer.

STRIPING A DRESSER

1 Apply base coat over gesso with roller or brush; start with lightest color. Let dry 1 hour, then repeat.

2 To create a stencil for remaining colors, use masking tape; press edges firmly for a tight seal.

3 Add stripes with three tints, beginning with the lightest color. Let the paint dry 1 hour each time.

4 Lift off the tape. Correct fuzzy edges, if needed, with a small, stiff-bristled brush.

Transformed with geometric pattern, ordinary chest and mirror have a bold, contemporary look.

Collage

Many decorative techniques are simply variations on the base coat/top glaze idea. Collage introduces paper into the works — and torn-up paper at that. (You buy craft paper at an artist's supply store or, in a pinch, use shelf paper from a variety store.)

Begin by priming all surfaces to be collaged. Then take time out for a paper-tearing party, reducing the craft or shelf paper to a pile of irregular shapes, as shown at right.

Glue paper shreds to the primed wood with wallpaper paste, smoothing and burnishing with your fingers. Overlap on some areas for a jagged, random effect. (Some artists prepaint the paper with stripes, spills, or directional swipes, then reorient fragments when positioning them on the furniture's surface.) Save straight-edged pieces for corners and furniture edges, or cut some clean edges for this purpose. Let the glue dry for at least several hours, then brush another coat of primer on top.

Next, apply a standard base coat, patting it on with a foam brush for a stippled effect; or use a paint roller with a long-napped roller cover. Again, let the piece dry.

Then, come back with a second, contrasting color, partially covering the base coat. Sponging, ragging, and other glazing techniques are all effective; we ragged on (see page 85) a latex wash (about 1 part paint to 1 part water) and let it dry overnight.

Finally, using medium-grit sandpaper, sand with a gentle circular motion, exposing the jagged, overlapping paper ridges below. Don't use a sanding block — it's too aggressive.

Protect the delicate paper from wear and tear by putting two coats of clear varnish over it.

FOUR COLLAGING STEPS

1 *Glue torn-up craft paper or shelf paper over primed wood, using wallpaper paste; burnish paper in place. Reprime atop paper.*

2 *Add base coat color, patting on paint with foam brush; or use long-napped paint roller for bumpy texture. Let surface dry thoroughly.*

3 *Apply second color over base coat, leaving gaps for base to show through. We mixed 1 part latex to 1 part water. Ragging on (page 85) is effective, especially with contrasting paint.*

4 *Let paint dry overnight, then gently sand through top coat and base coat to expose jagged paper edges. Use 150- or 180-grit sandpaper, sanding with circular motion.*

Crackling

Crackling is easy and fun — if you have the right materials for the job. Again, the process combines an opaque base coat and a contrasting top coat — with a layer of crackling glue between the two. The glue causes the top coat to stretch and crack, revealing the base coat though the gaps.

You can purchase crackling glue in art supply stores and some paint stores. Or try hot animal-hide glue (see page 28) or liquid hide glue. Some commercial products don't really do the trick, so you'll need to experiment or ask around.

Generally, the warmer your work space, the faster the surface will crackle. However, crackling can be tricky in some humid climates, as in the Southeastern states.

The process takes only a few minutes. A thick coat of glue tends to produce large cracks; using less glue is likely to result in finer detailing later.

Most crackling instructions recommend brushing on the top coat. But this introduces the possibility of smearing the softened glue as you work. It's safer to gently sponge on the top color, as shown at right.

We chose flat latex enamel for the base coat and semigloss for the top. But a range of other effects can be produced with washes and glazes. Use contrasting colors — light over dark or dark over light — for greatest visual drama.

Once your project has dried, apply a coat or two of clear varnish to protect against chipping. For an aged effect, tint the varnish slightly, as discussed on page 51.

CRACKLING A NIGHTSTAND

1 *Brush crackling glue over dry base coat; thick coat produces large cracks later, light coat produces finer patterns. Let glue dry about 1 hour.*

2 *Apply contrasting top coat over glue and base coat, dabbing it on with loaded sea sponge. Sponge method helps keep glue from smearing.*

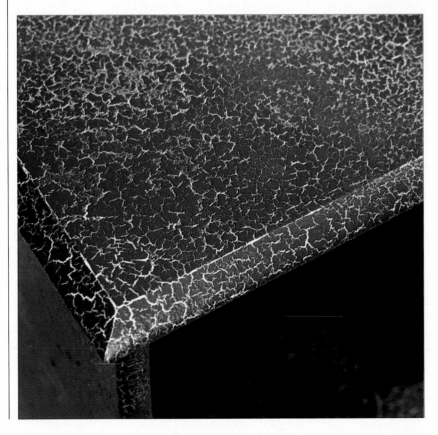

3 *The crackling process should occur within minutes. As glue resoftens, it stretches top emulsion, showing base coat color through gaps.*

Gilding

Gilding, or applying gold to wood, has been a decorative art for many centuries. In fact, some of the gilding techniques that were popular in ancient Egypt are still employed today.

Gold leaf is the most traditional material, but its high cost is often beyond the financial range of a beginning do-it-yourself finisher. Liquid gold-leaf paint, available at art supply and crafts stores, makes a relatively inexpensive substitute. Gold-leaf paint is most useful in small doses; if applied to large, flat surfaces, irregular brush marks will detract from the overall effect.

Wax gilding is also popular. Sold in cosmetic-type jars, this gold paste can easily be rubbed onto the wood surface (with one's fingers, a cloth, or a brush dipped in turpentine) and then buffed to a beautiful sheen. Gold wax can effectively freshen existing gilding and even out newly applied gold-leaf paint.

To prepare a smooth base for either leaf paint or wax, apply gesso (see page 92), sand it lightly when dry, then brush on a thin coat of shellac (see page 53). On many picture frames and furniture projects, the "new" gold look needs to be subdued or aged. Antiquing a gilt finish is like antiquing any other furniture finish (see pages 82–83).

For a large piece, you might want to buy gilding in dry form. It's sold as "booklets" of extremely thin pressed gold (really bronze), silver (aluminum), or copper sheets and is called *Dutch metal* or *composition leaf*. This is the material featured in the photos below.

GILDING A DRESSER

1 *First, paint on base coat: burnt sienna is traditional for gold leafing, navy blue for silver leafing. Then brush on "quick size" as shown, and let it dry for 1 hour. Size will remain tacky, forming base for leafing.*

2 *Apply gilding squares, burnishing with hand pressure. Metal crumbles easily, so wear a painter's mask. Repair holes and tears by rubbing on more metal. Dust metal into corners with soft-bristled brush. Finally, smooth surface nibs and edges with soft cloth.*

3 *For instant patina, spray with weak sodium sulfide/water mixture. Because of the smell, it's best to spray outdoors in the shade. Let dry 24 hours, then seal with alkyd varnish (water-based products will cloud surface). Expect intense colors to fade slightly.*

95

Index